LINCOLN CHRISTIAN COLLEG
P9-CMN-165

"David Chow goes beyond the shiny veneer of ministry and into the reality of our struggles. It's about time someone wrote a book like this."

—DAN KIMBALL
author of *The Emerging Church*

"*The Perfect Program* should be read by every youth worker who needs a dose of encouragement as well as reality. This will be the book I pass out to my youth ministry friends this year."

—JIM BURNS, PH.D.
president, HomeWord

"*The Perfect Program* strips away the dangerous and debilitating illusion of the superstar youth pastor. With playful candor and frightening accuracy, David Chow gives us an inside look in a way that invites us to lay aside the 'fairy tales' that have kept our ministries trapped in La La Land for far too long."

—MARK DEVRIES
founder, Youth Ministry Architects;
youth pastor, First Presbyterian Church, Nashville;
author of *Family-Based Youth Ministry*

"If you want to understand what an authentic leader looks like, read this book. David Chow candidly reminds us that personal failure and honest interaction with God are where true leadership grows. There is real wisdom in these pages. Read and become a better youth worker."

—DAN WEBSTER
founder, Authentic Leadership, Inc.

"The Perfect Program is refreshingly honest and real! David Chow has said what so many of us want to say but don't because we're afraid of letting down the 'ministry' mask. Get ready to be amused, challenged, and healed."

—FRED LYNCH
founder, GodStyle Productions; author of *The Epic*
founder, Authentic Leadership, Inc.

"David's insights are gritty, illuminating, and real without complaint or compromise. The power of God is made perfect in our weakness, not our programs."

—REV. CHRIS HILL
president, CHM International

THE
PERFECT
PROGRAM
and other fairy tales

DAVID CHOW

CONFESSIONS
of a well-intentioned
youth worker

TH1NK
P.O. Box 35001
Colorado Springs, Colorado 80935

© 2005 by David Chow

All rights reserved. No part of this publication may be reproduced in any form without written permission from NavPress, P.O. Box 35001, Colorado Springs, CO 80935.
www.navpress.com
TH1NK is an imprint of NavPress.
TH1NK and the TH1NK logo are registered trademarks of NavPress. Absence of ®
in connection with marks of NavPress or other parties does not indicate an absence of
registration of those marks.

ISBN 1-57683-822-6

Cover design by Disciple Design
Cover Photo: Getty Images
Creative Team: Nicci Jordan, Steve Parolini, Darla Hightower, Arvid Wallen, Glynese Northam

Unless otherwise identified, all Scripture quotations in this publication are taken from the
HOLY BIBLE: NEW INTERNATIONAL VERSION® (NIV®). Copyright © 1973, 1978, 1984 by
International Bible Society. Used by permission of Zondervan Publishing House. All rights
reserved. Other versions used include: THE MESSAGE (MSG). Copyright © 1993, 1994, 1995,
1996, 2000, 2001, 2002. Used by permission of NavPress Publishing Group; and the Holy
Bible, New Living Translation (NLT), copyright © 1996. Used by permission of Tyndale House
Publishers, Inc., Wheaton, Illinois 60189. All rights reserved.

Chow, David.
  The perfect program and other fairy tales : confessions of a
well-intentioned youth worker / David Chow.
     p. cm.
  Includes bibliographical references.
  ISBN 1-57683-822-6 (alk. paper)
  1. Church work with youth. I. Title.
  BV4447.C4772 2005
  259'.23--dc22
                              2005022497

Printed in Canada

1 2 3 4 5 6 7 8 9 10 / 09 08 07 06 05

FOR A FREE CATALOG OF
NAVPRESS BOOKS & BIBLE STUDIES,
CALL 1-800-366-7788 (USA)
OR 1-800-839-4769 (CANADA)

Contents

753

112277

Acknowledgments

I owe the following people special thanks. Without them, this book would never have become what it is.

To Lori Chow, my wonderful and incredible wife, who faithfully supported me throughout the process of writing, editing, rewriting, and editing again. I don't know what I would have done without you.

To my editor, Steve Parolini, who stretched and challenged me to write in such a way that was authentic and engaging to others. Your input and editing took this book to a higher level.

To Jay Howver, who helped me gain a clearer vision for this book. Instead of writing from the "head," you encouraged me to write from the "heart," making it much more personal and emotional.

Introduction

Make this your common practice:
Confess your sins to each other and pray for each other
so that you can live together whole and healed.
The prayer of a person living right with God
is something powerful to be reckoned with.

— James 5:16, *MSG*

WANT SOME ADVICE? Don't become a "youth expert."

What's a youth expert? Someone who's put many years into youth work; someone who's led youth ministry at a well-known church; someone who gets asked to speak at conferences; someone who's written a book or two on the subject.

That's how I became one.

But it's not all red carpets and limos. When I was tagged "youth expert," suddenly I could no longer be a bumbling youth worker. I could no longer struggle with uncertainty, insecurity, and discouragement. I was supposed to have all the answers.

I can't speak for other youth ministry experts, but *I* don't have all the answers.

This book is my confession of that truth. It's packed with

my failures, fears, and confusion, along with just a smattering of triumphs, successes, and accomplishments. I'm putting into practice James 5:16: "Therefore confess your sins to each other and pray for each other so that you may be healed." True healing only comes from "coming clean" before God, others, and with myself. You might say this book is essentially for me — that it's my own little therapy session — but it may be yours as well.

My hope is that after reading about my journey, you will discuss, debate, and discern the true definition of ministry success. I don't write as someone who has arrived or has figured it all out; I write as a wounded-healer on a journey toward authentic, biblical ministry. I wrote this book to proclaim, "Here's how I did it wrong and what I'm learning from it." This book isn't about giving you the right answers but about helping you ask the right questions. It isn't about refining how you do ministry but about helping you reflect on ministry. And it's not about reaching a destination; it's about starting a journey of loving and reaching teenagers, a journey of discovering who you are as a leader, a journey of leading together with others, and most importantly, a journey with Jesus.

01 PERFECT PROGRAM

For we know in part and we prophesy in part, but when
perfection comes, the imperfect disappears. When I was
a child, I talked like a child, I thought like a child, I
reasoned like a child. When I became a man,
I put childish ways behind me.
— 1 Corinthians 13:9-11

I THOUGHT I COULD ACHIEVE PERFECTION.

My entry into youth ministry began as most new jobs do, with a motivating blend of hope and fear and equal measures of confidence and ignorance. Ignorance kicked in first as I fumbled around in my new role as youth pastor, initially just trying to figure out how to work with students. In many ways it was freeing and exciting as I had to rely on God and trust him to fill in where I was weak. But excitement turned into anxiety as time moved me from "it's okay that you don't know what you're doing—you're still new" to "you should really know what you're doing by now." The longer I was a youth pastor, the more I felt it necessary to know what I was doing. And not only that, the more I felt it necessary to *excel* at what I was doing. Call it wide-eyed optimism, arrogance, or a simple faith that God would honor my efforts, but I wanted to develop a program that others would look at with awe. Anything less wasn't good enough.

Not having been formally trained in youth ministry, I wanted to learn as much as I could about it. I read every youth ministry book I could find, attended as many youth ministry conferences as I could afford, and began talking to as many youth workers as possible. It wasn't long before I noticed a common theme: Instead of having a *model* for ministry, youth workers were "flying by the seat of their pants" looking for the next big idea or guaranteed-to-succeed event. I wasn't going to fall into this trap — I would have a model. A perfect one.

LOOKING FOR THE HOLY GRAIL

At my first youth ministry conference — a Youth Specialties Youthworker Convention — I was encouraged, inspired, and overwhelmed, and I found myself agreeing with everything I heard. I entered this career with a simplistic understanding of youth ministry. I mean, how hard could it be hanging out with teenagers and telling them about Jesus for a couple hours a week? My simple understanding was exploded by the barrage of ministry methods and styles and approaches presented at the convention — each one offering nuggets of wisdom I needed to know. Wanting desperately to find a clear and unifying understanding of youth ministry, I convinced myself that with enough effort and diligence

I could develop a program that blended the best elements of all the different youth ministry approaches and systems.

I would create . . . "the perfect program."

But I didn't have enough to work with after just one convention. There was much more to learn. I was just getting started.

After the Youth Specialties conference, I signed up for a Sonlife Ministries seminar. There I studied Scripture passage after Scripture passage to discover how Jesus had led his ministry. As much as I believed in Jesus, it had never occurred to me to look to him for how to run a youth program. Well, I certainly wanted my youth program to be biblically grounded, so I soaked up all I could about Jesus' ministry. A perfect youth ministry program would certainly follow in the footsteps of Jesus.

Unfortunately, while the seminar was helpful in encouraging me to think more biblically about youth ministry, it left a lot of questions unanswered. It turns out the Bible doesn't include many details on how Jesus organized camps and retreats and lock-ins and fund-raising dinners, or led crazy games and engaging worship. And, disappointingly, it doesn't include a template for a monthly calendar that you can fill in with program details and send off to students and parents. Because the seminar didn't provide a methodology for youth ministry, I left still searching for the perfect youth program.

The next place I turned was to a well-respected youth ministry expert you've probably heard of: Jim Burns. Jim had been a successful youth pastor (he was Doug Field's youth pastor) and the author of several youth ministry books. In his book *Youthbuilder,* Jim emphasized the importance of the practical side of youth ministry, such as learning how to teach creatively, plan camps and mission trips, do relational ministry, and help kids in crisis. Of course! This was *clearly* the missing link for my perfect youth program. The perfect youth program must include both a biblical foundtion *and* a practical element.

Several months later, I went to one of Jim's youth ministry conferences. Many of the things I had already heard from Jim and read in *Youthbuilder* were reinforced at the conference. But at this event I also discovered a youth pastor named Doug Fields. At the time, Doug was a full-time speaker and had yet to go to Saddleback Church. He spent a day sharing with us his model for youth ministry, what would later become the basis for his best-selling book *Purpose-Driven Youth Ministry*. Doug shared about the importance of having a *purpose* for your youth program and how too many youth workers focus on the "what" of youth ministry before they focus on the "why." He argued that when youth workers don't know why their youth programs exist, they lack direction and purpose. He proposed that the starting point for any youth program should be a clear purpose statement that highlights the importance of evangelism, discipleship, worship, fellowship, and service.

I couldn't adequately answer the question, "Why does our youth program exist?" so I was deeply convicted of the need to have a purpose statement. I went back to my church and labored over the process, crafting the exact wording and coming up with the perfect purpose statement. With a new passion for having a purpose-driven youth ministry, I spent several months communicating our purpose to students, parents, and church leaders. I put our purpose statement everywhere: in the youth room, on our church brochure, on youth ministry newsletters and calendars, in our volunteer packet, and in the youth room restroom!

I was certain that *now* I had combined all of the components into the perfect youth program. That is, until I came across a book in the local Christian bookstore titled *Family-Based Youth Ministry* by Mark DeVries. I was especially intrigued by an endorsement by Jim Burns: "This is the book we have been waiting for . . . moving us from a 'traditional youth ministry' to a different style of youth work that is desperately needed." I purchased the book and immediately went home to read it. The book critiqued the problems with a traditional youth ministry model and how youth ministries were losing relevance and impact with today's youth. It went on to argue that because youth workers have ignored the importance of the biological as well as the church family, they have created youth ministries that isolate students from adults. As a consequence, youth ministries had become increasingly ineffective at helping students develop a lifelong faith, form connections with the larger church, and serve faithfully in the body of Christ.

Because I agreed with much of what the book had to say, I began to question everything I had learned about youth ministry. I asked myself questions such as "Why hadn't I learned this before? I don't remember Jesus having to work with parents. Is 'family ministry' another purpose of the church?" This wasn't a book that argued for new ways of *doing* youth ministry, it argued for a whole new way of *thinking about* youth ministry.

I tried to put all the pieces together as I began incorporating many of the concepts into my program. I had to start acknowledging that parents really are the most powerful influence in the lives of students. I had to admit that I was relying on my youth ministry programs and events to help my students grow spiritually instead of finding ways to connect students to their families as well as to the family of God. I started focusing more energy on supporting and empowering parents to spiritually nurture their children.

Though my introduction to family-based youth ministry had caught me off guard, I was convinced I could still make it work. And so I began leading a biblically grounded, purpose-driven, family-based youth program. After considerable success at one church, I felt I had finally accomplished my goal. Parents were empowered, students were growing in their faith, the whole church was involved, and everything had a purpose and biblical foundation. I had created the perfect program.

WHEN MINISTRY GOT MESSY

Everything came crashing down when I went to my next church. I knew I would face many challenges based on the history of the youth group, but I never anticipated that I would face the challenge of having to learn how to do youth ministry all over again.

I had never ministered in a lower-income, urban, working-class community where the majority of people were Hispanic or Asian. This was a distinct contrast to my previous churches.

There, the communities consisted of primarily white, middle-class, suburban families. Because I had grown up in a similar middle-class community, it was relatively easy for me to connect with and understand the students I worked with. In this new church, I was working with students who came from a completely different background and were dealing with many at-risk issues. More than half of our students lived in single-parent homes, many were struggling to graduate from high school, and others were falling prey to teen pregnancy, juvenile delinquency, abuse, and suicide. I struggled to connect with my students and their issues.

Teaching had always been a strength of my ministry, but suddenly it was a weakness. The students I was working with were so different from students I had worked with in the past, I didn't know how to relate the Bible to their lives. Messages that had been received positively in my previous churches were met with yawns, confused looks, or unruly behavior. It didn't matter whether I was speaking on sex, the end times, or whether there is sex in the end times, students were not connecting with my teaching.

Youth camps had always been well attended and a powerful catalyst for changing lives and creating community. Thinking that this was just what this group needed, I poured time and energy into our first winter camp. Despite promoting the camp for several months, only a handful of students signed up. And for the first time in my ministry career, we canceled a camp. I couldn't believe this had happened. I was depressed and disappointed.

Family ministry had also previously been a wonderful success. Parents enthusiastically attended workshops, intergenerational events, and parent meetings. Now, I was having a hard time getting anyone involved or even interested in family ministry. At my quarterly parent meetings, I was lucky to have one person show up, even after sending out letters and personally contacting parents. My family ministry events didn't fare much better; I must have promoted our first parent-teen event for over a month. It was a disaster of the Hindenburg scale. We had fewer parents there than volunteers.

It was the last parent-teen event we did for a very long time.

Special events weren't working either. I thought a well-advertised all-nighter would produce the excitement and momentum we needed. I wasn't prepared for the lack of enthusiasm or the complaints by students that followed. Then there was the "October Eve" event on Halloween. I organized this event as an outreach to the community: bringing in a DJ, an inflatable bungee run, a boxing ring, and lots of free food. But all the advertising, attention, and preparation had very little impact on who came or whether they enjoyed the night. Many of the students who showed up just sat around, refusing to participate in the night's activities. Others complained that they would rather be trick-or-treating.

As a last-ditch effort to force-fit my perfect-program model into this new church, I came up with a super event titled "Outrageous October." I would take the entire month of October and offer a high-energy, themed event every week. There was food night, sports night, "glow" night, and Luau night. In keeping with tradition, we went all out and elaborately decorated the room each week and promised all sorts of prizes and giveaways for students. To top things off, we promised a free Xbox to the person who brought the most friends over the course of the month.

Outrageous October was a success as students came week after week, had a fun time, and went away with lots of free stuff. I was feeling pretty good about myself — my perfect program was working once again. Then Outrageous October became Nosedive November. The week after we ended our outreach month, attendance fell through the floor. At first, I thought students would eventually come back, but they never did.

MY IMPERFECT YOUTH PROGRAM

I finally had to admit that my perfect program wasn't perfect. It certainly wasn't "one size fits all." I had believed that doing youth ministry the same way at every church would result in the same success. But it took me nearly two years of beating my head against the wall to realize this wasn't true. I spent the next few years trying to figure out a new way to do youth ministry.

The big lesson: There is *no such thing* as a perfect youth program — no such thing as "perfect ministry." Ministry by definition is imperfect, unpredictable, and unwieldy. Youth ministry is much more complicated and a lot messier than seminars and all those great youth ministry books make it seem. And as I thought about Jesus' ministry, I realized that while he may have had a strategy for ministry, he was always adapting and flexing with the situations and people he came into contact with. Jesus never prescribed that we all do ministry the same way.

The other problem was that my ministry model didn't leave room for creativity and innovation. Because my perfect program was based on a set of assumptions and beliefs and had been successful in the past, thinking outside of the box was almost impossible. As much as I valued innovation and prided myself on being a creative leader, I was having a difficult time trying anything new or different. I didn't recognize this problem when everything was working well, but it became obvious when I tried changing the way I did youth ministry. Just because God had blessed my way of doing ministry in the past didn't mean he would do it again. As tempting as it was for me to go into "autopilot," God wanted me to keep on my toes and be sensitive to his leading.

I don't want to diminish all that I have learned from the different ministry approaches — the books, the seminars, the experts. We need them all. But I hit a wall when I put my trust in the perfect program instead of the perfect God. It was only after giving up on having the perfect youth program that I could accept and embrace ministry for what it ultimately really was — caring for people, not just carrying out a plan.

02 Perfect Calling

If I proclaim the Message, it's not to get something out of it for myself. I'm compelled to do it, and doomed if I don't! If this was my own idea of just another way to make a living, I'd expect some pay. But since it's not my idea but something solemnly entrusted to me, why would I expect to get paid?
— 1 Corinthians 9:16-17, MSG

I DIDN'T WANT TO BE A YOUTH PASTOR. I WANTED TO BE psychologist. Or a paramedic.

I planned to follow up my degree in psychology with graduate school and become a clinical psychologist. That was Plan One. I had a backup plan, too. I could become a paramedic at an ambulance company where I had been working part-time if the whole "clinical psychology" thing didn't work out.

Youth ministry was not Plan Three. Or Four. Or anywhere on the list.

Everything changed when my fiancée, Lori, asked, "Have you thought about working for the church?"

"Why would I want to do that?"

"It's just a thought."

Just a thought. Yeah, a thought that would eventually change my life.

I had no idea what it meant to "work for the church." I was aware it didn't pay well because the interns I knew had to raise their own financial support. Do all people who go into ministry take a vow of poverty? I had a hard time seeing myself working for a church. I assumed people who went into ministry knew right away that that was what they were supposed to do. Brian, a friend from college, knew from the day I met him he wanted to be a youth pastor. I don't know if Brian had a burning bush or Damascus road experience like Moses or Paul, but he knew early on that that's what God had called him to do. Immediately after graduating from college he took a youth pastor job.

I never heard that call.

Growing up in a family that didn't attend church, I had gone to church maybe once or twice. But during high school, a friend invited me to the youth group and I began going on a regular basis. I became a Christian in my junior year of high school, and while I sincerely believed that everyone should become a Christian, I sure didn't think everyone should become a pastor. The role of pastor was reserved for super-spiritual individuals who had a special connection to God — something I didn't have.

Still, I couldn't get Lori's question out of my mind. "Have I ever thought of working for the church?"

While working a twenty-four-hour ambulance shift, I told

my partner Sam I was considering applying for an internship in the college group of my church instead of going full-time at the ambulance company. Sam was not a Christian. He loved to egg me on by continually swearing around me and making inappropriate comments. One time while working a shift together, he asked me to go into a convenience store to buy him a copy of *Penthouse* magazine. After I refused, he went into the store to buy the magazine while I hid behind the steering wheel.

I knew Sam's views on religion, and I was sure he would discourage me from working for the church. To my surprise, he shared that if he could do things over, he wouldn't have rushed into getting a "real job" and instead would have done something more interesting and adventurous. He told me this was a unique time for me to pursue opportunities I wouldn't be able to later.

That's all I needed to hear. I applied for the intern position and eventually was accepted into the program at my church.

PERFECT EXPECTATIONS

"It will be great!" I told my friends. "I can't wait to start working for my church. Just imagine how much I'll grow in my faith. It will be *perfect*."

There was that word again.

Maybe I was reading the Bible too much or taking sermons too seriously, but I had this vision of working for the church as a nonstop prayer and Bible study meeting. It would be like going to camp every week—except, fortunately, without the camp food. I expected every staff member would be like Mother Teresa or Billy Graham or Mr. Rogers, and we would all spend the majority of our time praying and studying the Bible.

Who knew that pastors had to go to meetings, fill out paperwork, and submit annual budgets? I vividly remember my first planning meeting where we spent hours discussing future church events and programs as well as a host of ministry ideas. Though unspoken, my thoughts were probably quite transparent to the rest of the staff.

"This is *so boring*. Jesus didn't go to staff meetings, so why do I have to go?"

I wasn't prepared for the administration involved in ministry. I struggled to get my required staff reports in every week; I think I succeeded about half the time. At staff meetings, they would pass out request cards from students asking for information, prayer, and personal follow-up. Week after week I would let my cards pile up. I collected enough unresponded cards that I could've built a bonfire with them. But a bonfire wouldn't have burned away the guilt I felt about not praying for these students.

To compound my struggle with the administrative side of ministry, I had some unspoken expectations of the internship. I expected that my college pastor, Dan, would disciple me. I thought that the main purpose of the internship was for him to help me grow spiritually. I know that wasn't written anywhere on the paperwork I signed or in my job description, but somehow I thought that's how it worked. No one had ever discipled me before—no one had invested in my spiritual growth in that way, and I longed for that.

Oh, we met weekly, but it wasn't what I expected. Dan would ask how I was doing and how my ministry projects were going. Although he was genuinely interested in how I was doing, it was obvious that we were meeting more to review ministry tasks than we were to "get spiritual" and help me grow as a Christian. Unfortunately, I never vocalized my desires to be discipled by him. If I had, he surely would have taken the time or would have connected me with someone who could.

I realize now that it was unfair for me to expect this from Dan. While I know he was more than capable of doing this, I was brought on staff primarily to serve and lead others, not to be discipled. I know now that I'm ultimately responsible for my spiritual growth and to expect him to take responsibility for that was unfair.

RAISING SUPPORT

Depending on God for my financial needs was difficult. I lacked the confidence to approach people asking for their help. As a result, I was not very good at raising support. I chose to keep my job at the ambulance company to help make ends meet. While I'm sure there was some measure of wisdom in choosing to continue my work there, I see now that it was also an easy way for me to avoid the challenge of raising full support for my internship — and an easy way to sidestep the need to trust God in this.

Time and a growing faith built my confidence in approaching people, and eventually I developed my financial base so I no longer needed to work at the ambulance company. As people gave willingly and joyfully to me, I learned a critical lesson about finances: All money is God's money. I also realized that I'm called to share my resources with others as well. Because I had been on the receiving end, I found it easier to give to others as I had been given to.

The internship was nearing an end, and though it had been a good experience, I was still convinced God wanted me to become a Christian psychologist.

But when the next year came, I found myself applying once again to be an intern.

I almost didn't get accepted back. I had offended some people, including the youth pastor, because of my deficiencies as a "team player." Dan was working with me through these issues, but it was still a risk for him to bring me back. By God's grace, he asked me back for another year with an understanding that I needed to work harder at getting along with other staff and knowing when to keep my mouth shut.

I did a little better the next year.

I'm thankful Dan took a chance on me, because if he hadn't, I probably wouldn't have continued in ministry. I would have been a psychologist. Or a paramedic.

But here I am, still doing ministry nearly fifteen years later.

THE CALLING OF YOUTH MINISTRY

I could argue that God arranged it so I would choose youth ministry over graduate school the next year. But, actually, I sort of arranged that by my own laziness. Because I had procrastinated on taking my GREs, I wasn't eligible to apply for graduate school. So what else could I do? I decided to take a youth ministry position.

My first youth group night taught me a thing or two about how different it is to work with teenagers. It was a Tuesday night — the night for the junior high group. The pastor had told me to expect about forty junior highers. Having come from a college group with more than two hundred students, I assumed I could easily handle forty junior highers. After all, they were *only* junior highers. (I hear all of you seasoned youth workers snickering. You know what's coming.)

When I walked in and saw the energy level in the room, I started to panic. The boys were running around, chasing after and yelling at each other like lions, each vying for the "king of the jungle" role. One of the girls was chasing the boys too, but I think for different reasons. The rest of the girls were hanging out among themselves and making fun of the boys. After a short introduction by the pastor, he left.

And I was suddenly alone with forty junior highers.

Things went pretty well during the first part of the night as I shared a little about myself and how I came to faith. I started running into problems when I tried to lead my first game.

There's a big difference between explaining something to a college student and to a junior higher. Part of the problem is the attention span of junior highers. When I first gave the instructions, I spent a long time talking about the purpose of the game, what would happen if students broke the rules, and all the specific details of the activity. By the time I was done, everyone was looking at me with blank expressions. Then the questions came, in rapid-fire succession.

"What are we supposed to be doing?"

"Why are there so many rules?"

"Can you explain it to us again?"

"Can we play another game?"

It got worse. During the "teaching time," I discovered that, unlike the college students I had taught who had found my lessons "deep and challenging," my junior highers found them deeply challenging to pay any attention to. The students that weren't asleep were bouncing off the walls, talking to each other, and shooting spit wads onto the ceiling.

I felt like a substitute teacher being eaten alive by a pack of piranhas. At first, I waited for the students to calm down, assuming they would figure out on their own that it was time to pay attention. That didn't work. I tried reasoning with them by explaining the importance of my lesson, why they needed to listen, and how they needed to pay attention. That didn't work.

So I tried begging and pleading. Nope.

Finally, I resorted to prayer. As you can imagine, I wasn't getting anywhere. Fortunately, one of the volunteers, who also happened to be a kindergarten teacher, came to my rescue and managed to get them calmed down. God bless her!

I can't remember whether I finished my lesson or not, but I do remember one painfully vivid question I asked myself, "What have I gotten myself into?"

Over the coming weeks and months, I learned many lessons about working with teens. One of the first was that if I planned to work with teenagers long-term, I would need to have a "calling" to do so. After all, what sane and emotionally stable individual would want to devote his life to working with "insane" and "emotionally driven" teenagers? I realized that if I didn't have a calling to work with youth, I should get out while I had the chance. I certainly didn't want to take it out on the students if I wasn't called to work with them.

I actually liked working with teenagers more than working with college students. Teens were a lot more work, but at the same time, they were much more moldable. I was amazed to see how hungry and open they were for someone to invest in them and take them seriously. Whether it was picking them up after school, hanging out after youth group, or going to their school events, I enjoyed my time with students.

After eight months in the job, I came to a startling conclusion —I loved working with teenagers, and I couldn't see myself doing anything else. The idea of being a Christian psychologist was rapidly losing appeal as I realized that my interests, gifts, and passions fit better with youth ministry.

I didn't find my calling . . . my calling found me.

I told my pastor I desired to go full-time and stay long-term so I could dedicate more time and energy to developing the youth ministry. He was open to me staying long-term, but bringing me on full-time wasn't in their plans. Even though they had the resources to do so, they wanted to allocate them elsewhere. I decided to resign and seek a full-time position.

I don't think that was the wisest decision. Although I didn't leave out of anger or with a desire to hurt anyone, I should have taken more time and been more sensitive to the church's situation and needs. I was young and impatient, and moved on too quickly. The church was gracious with my departure, and, ironically, they did end up hiring a full-time youth pastor a year later.

Amazingly, God led me to another church within just a few weeks.

A GROWING CALLING

Youth ministry became something I lived and breathed as God's call on my life. And even though I was making lots of mistakes, I was motivated to find more effective ways to reach students and help them grow in their faith. I knew my sense of calling was growing because instead of tiring of youth ministry, I became more and more passionate about it. But I had yet to be tested in a significant way.

The first test came when our youth group started reaching a large number of unchurched students. Because we were growing faster than I could recruit staff or develop student leaders, our group morphed into one made up of mostly non-Christians. As exciting as it was to have so many non-Christians, it created a lot of problems. There were issues with discipline, bullying, and the free flow of obscenities around the room. And these were the junior highers! I had to play the role of "bad guy"—at least that's probably how many students saw me as I enforced discipline and occasionally asked disrespectful students to leave. During these tougher times, my calling reminded me that reaching and loving students was more important than being liked by them—even if this meant being unpopular for setting appropriate boundaries.

Some parents were unhappy with me, too, during this out-of-control growth season. While most parents had been supportive of me when the youth group was smaller and made up primarily of churched students, some began to criticize my work and even accuse me of things that weren't true. One parent accused me of naming our junior high youth group "Breakaway" because I wanted teenagers to "breakaway and rebel" against their parents.

Somehow I kept from becoming discouraged or even bitter toward these parents. I didn't like upsetting anyone, but I felt I had to follow God's leading and not the expectations of others. As much as I wanted people to be happy with me, I had to follow my call to reach and love teenagers. It was during times like this that my calling provided the strength and support I needed to do what was right even if it was unpopular.

As important as my calling is to me, I've had to learn that because people express their calling in different ways, it's unfair for me to expect others to view ministry the way I do. One of my youth ministry friends helped me understand this. He's just as passionate about his call to youth ministry as I am, but he expresses his calling through faithfully being there for his students. Never too busy for them, he ministers to students whether they are in the hospital, in jail, or out on the street. While he probably won't be remembered for his sermons or special events, he will be remembered for his presence and relational commitment to his students.

A children's pastor I worked with also helped me understand this. She was just as passionate about children's ministry as I was about youth ministry. Her calling was seen more in her commitment to discipleship, careful planning, and quality programming. Over time, we learned to work together as we both understood the unique ways in which we expressed our calling. She told me later, "You weren't always easy to get along with, but you were always easy to work with." What she meant was that even though our differences resulted in conflict, because we both had a clear calling and vision for ministry, we always had a common denominator.

KEEPING MY CALLING CLEAR

Calling can become lost in the clutter when passion becomes profession. When the challenges of the job — and, yes, it is also a job — start to mount, it's tempting to lead with your head instead of your heart. This happened to me when I became more concerned about being a competent professional than being a passionate leader. I had to remind myself that, while both are important, being passionate in ministry is always more important than being professional in ministry.

There's another risk to losing your calling, and that's becoming comfortable. A calling — a passion for ministry — gives courage to face opposition and challenge. Choosing comfort over a continuing passion leads to a loss of vision. For this reason, courage always needs to take precedence over comfort. I appreciate what Andy Stanley has to say about courage in ministry:

> *A leader is someone who has the courage to say publicly what everybody else is whispering privately. It is not his insight that sets the leader apart from the crowd. It is his courage to act on what he sees, to speak up when everyone else is silent. Next generation leaders are those that would rather challenge what needs to change and pay the price than remain silent and die on the inside.[1]*

There's one more thing that can derail your calling — focusing on the idea of career above all else. If I become more focused on building my resume than on building the kingdom, if I worry about how much vacation I receive, what kind of benefits I get, and whether or not each opportunity will advance my career, I'll miss the big picture. I'll lose sight of what defined youth ministry as my calling in the first place. It's during these times that God has to bring me back to the words of Paul in 1 Corinthians 9:16-17:

> *Yet when I preach the gospel, I cannot boast, for I am compelled to preach. Woe to me if I do not preach the gospel! If I preach voluntarily, I have a reward; if not voluntarily, I am simply discharging the trust committed to me.*

03 Perfect Drive

I do all this for the sake of the gospel,
that I may share in its blessings.
Do you not know that in a race all the runners run,
but only one gets the prize?
Run in such a way as to get the prize.
Everyone who competes in the games goes into strict training.
They do it to get a crown that will not last;
but we do it to get a crown that will last forever.
— 1 Corinthians 9:23-25

MORE SLEEP, MORE VACATIONS, MORE CAFFEINE, AND MORE determination weren't cutting it anymore. My endless supply of youthful zeal and passion was coming to an end. I could feel my body moving and my mouth speaking, but the rest of me was stuck. On the outside, I looked like I was busy and fulfilled, but on the inside, I was slowing down and becoming discouraged. Five years into ministry and I was suffering from a severe case of burnout.

This wasn't the first time I had encountered exhaustion in ministry. In college ministry, it was normal for me to feel fatigued and exhausted toward the end of the semester and school year. However, these times were short-lived and offered natural breaks between semesters and during the summer when I could slow down and unplug. I always had enough time to rest and recharge my batteries.

But this was different. Despite all my efforts, the feelings persisted.

At first, it was difficult for me to fathom that such a thing could happen. When I started in ministry, you couldn't pull me away from my job. I couldn't believe the church was actually paying me to do what I used to do for free. I remember telling Lori how much the church was going to pay me and almost feeling guilty about it. Okay, it wasn't *that* much money, but from my perspective, just paying me anything to work with teenagers was exciting. Yes, I would have done it for free.

My first few years in ministry were full of excitement and energy. I wanted to spend time with my students every day. I would hang out with students after school, watch them compete or perform in extracurricular activities, or have them stop by to raid my refrigerator. My wife and I lived down the street from the church so students could come over whenever they wanted. It was energizing for us to share our home and lives with students.

I had this habit of inviting a bunch of guys over to the house for video game all-nighters. Shortly after the original Sony PlayStation was released, we had a group over to test out the latest and greatest video game system. Consuming lots of pizza and soda, we battled all night to see who would become the reigning video game champion. The next morning, the living room looked like a grenade had hit it, with food shrapnel scattered across the floor amid unconscious students still clutching their video game controllers. Lori and I cherished times like this because we never felt a need to have a sharp separation between "work" and our "personal life." Work *was* our personal life. We saw ministry as our calling.

There weren't enough hours in a day to do all that I wanted in my job. No one had to force me to go to work; I loved being there. The many hours I spent preparing Bible studies, planning special events, and making fliers and newsletters raced by as I gave myself over to my work. This was before the days of desktop publishing, so many of those hours were spent picking out the perfect clip art, physically cutting and pasting the clip art onto paper, making photocopies, folding them, stamping them, and then mailing them off to students. Despite all the hard work, I felt great joy as I saw the newsletter going out in the mail.

Before I went into ministry, I hated reading and studying. But after entering the ministry, I couldn't learn enough about theology, biblical principles, and issues facing teenagers. Motivated by a desire to honor God and the students I taught, I wanted to give my best. Even though I would teach two or three times a week, I always had enough energy to work on another lesson or Bible study.

THE CHANGE

But soon I was exhausted and tired of being around students. I barely had the energy to connect with them at church. I began to avoid the neediest students at youth group. Instead of making myself available to listen and empathize with them, I kept myself occupied with ministry tasks, such as organizing the room, preparing the game, or getting ready for my Bible study. I had even less energy outside of church, and I found myself spending less and less time with students beyond our weekly programs or special events. I began to make excuses about why I couldn't go to the school campus or hang out with them. I even started rescheduling some of my one-on-one discipleship meetings.

One student I was discipling, Scott, was getting frustrated because I kept canceling more meetings than we were actually having. I didn't want to let him down, but I didn't have the heart to tell him I needed a break from meeting every week. So he suffered through the summer thinking I wanted to meet, but actually meeting only a handful of times. My actions weren't matching my words and Scott was one of many who suffered for that.

It became harder and harder for me to prepare Bible studies and youth talks. While I had once loved to research and study for my lessons, now I found myself relying more and more on curriculum. I didn't use curriculum as a "starting place" for a meeting, I pretty much just followed it verbatim so I wouldn't have to prepare. My students could tell something was wrong when they started noticing the words "photocopy reproducible" on the bottom of handouts. If the curriculum was too difficult to work with or I was struggling with it, I resorted to the well-tested and completely faulty youth ministry method that had sent me toward creating the perfect program years before: flying by the seat of my pants. I made up the lesson as I went along. When things were *really* bad, I showed videos. The audible groans that filled the room every time I popped in another *Edge TV*, Ken Davis, or Mr. Bean video soon signaled I'd overused this time-filling tactic. I resorted to one final approach: I planned long games so my message could be short.

Through all this, I lost perspective. I became irritated and frustrated over the smallest mistakes. At our annual summer camping trip, I went ballistic after I found out upon arrival that we had forgotten to buy hamburger buns for dinner. Instead of going with the flow and dealing with more important issues like setting up the tents and helping everyone focus on the purpose of the camp, I reacted like it was the end of the world and that the camp was all a waste of time and now was doomed to fail. All over hamburger buns!

The weekend turned out to be one of our most powerful camps ever, but because I was burned out, I couldn't see the bigger picture of what God wanted to do.

Somewhere in the middle of this burnout season, I shared my feelings of exhaustion with a fellow youth worker who had been in ministry about as long as I.

"I'm feeling the same way and I can't seem to shake the feeling either," he said.

Sitting there staring at each other, it was obvious we didn't have a clue what was going on or what to do about it. After this conversation, I assumed it was normal to feel this way in ministry and that I just had to ride it out.

The longer this went on, the more I began to feel dissatisfied with my church. I began to think things like "If my senior pastor were different I wouldn't feel this unhappy"; "If the church supported the youth ministry more, I wouldn't be frustrated and discouraged"; "If the church were reaching new families, I wouldn't have to work so hard at reaching new students"; and "If certain students would *stop* coming to youth group, things would go so much more smoothly." I started focusing on all the negative things about the church, convincing myself that all my feelings and problems would go away if I went to a different church.

Blaming the church was an easy way for me to explain why I felt the way I did. A new church with a new senior pastor and new students was all that I needed. To make matters worse, this was happening while our church was dealing with a financial crisis. Burnout coupled with my disillusionment over how the financial crisis was being handled—I took the easy way out.

I left.

At the time, I felt totally right about my choice and that God had led me to such a decision. It was only during the transition time between churches that I started to realize I might have made a rash decision. After having ample time to rest, reflect, and heal, my perspective changed as I realized how I had let burnout influence my judgment. My problem had been an internal issue, not an external one. Through this realization of the power of burnout, God taught me some important lessons.

LESSONS LEARNED

I learned the hard lesson that my youthful energy couldn't sustain ministry indefinitely. I thought I was immune from burnout, but I learned that just as there is a honeymoon period in marriage where emotions and exhilaration run high, there is a honeymoon period in ministry where the excitement and zeal of ministry carry you.

Unlike many other occupations, there isn't an easily accessible "off switch" for youth ministry. My wife could come home and be done with her work for the day, but for me work continued after I stepped through the front door. There was always more ministry to do: another student to hang out with, another letter to write, another Bible study to prepare, or another special event or camp to plan. Because ministry had no clear boundaries and my work kept expanding, I did ministry nonstop.

I needed to put better boundaries on my work at church.

One resolution I made was to start taking regular days off. In the past, I would only take days off when I was physically exhausted. Drawing on my past experience with sports helped me to put things into perspective. I recalled a basic principle of training — if I wanted to perform at my best, I needed to regularly and consistently take time off so my body could heal and rest. I began to see my days off not as an escape from work, but as a time to renew and refocus so I could return to ministry more revived and recharged.

It was during my time off between churches when I realized that I had confused growing a ministry with growing spiritually. I enjoyed spending time with God, studying and memorizing the Bible, and surrounding myself with people who challenged and encouraged me in the faith. But after I entered ministry, I unconsciously switched my focus from growing closer to God to becoming a better servant for God.

Like the story of Mary and Martha in Luke 10, I started out as Mary, but over time, became more like Martha. Consumed with the work of God, I substituted Bible study preparation for reading the Bible devotionally, leading prayer meetings for personal prayer, and running a youth group for spiritual accountability and fellowship. Like Martha, I allowed the work of ministry to become more important than the work of God in my own life. Unlike Mary, I spent more time doing things for God than I did sitting at his feet. I burned out because I was paying attention to everyone else's spiritual needs, but not my own.

After reading the book *The Godbearing Life*, I realized I wasn't alone in my struggle. I was especially encouraged by the following words:

> *After a few years of ministry — three to be exact — the programs I worked with began to seem weary. . . . If God had me gung-ho, God also made me tired — and not just because I needed more sleep. My soul was on empty; I was running on fumes, and the ministry entrusted to my care was too. The depressing truth was that youth were not the only ones who needed more substantial faith; so did I.* [2]

While the book didn't solve my problems, it did validate my struggles. I had forgotten to feed my own soul in the process of feeding everyone else's. I started paying closer attention to my own spiritual and emotional needs. I also reached out to others who could encourage me and keep me accountable. And I reminded myself constantly that God "works *in* me before he works *through* me."

As I reflected on my burnout, I began to understand why the average youth pastor only stays in ministry for three to five years. I had assured myself that this statistic wouldn't apply to me because I was different, and I had uncovered a "calling" for ministry. Instead, I was on the verge of becoming another statistic myself.

I wish I could tell you that I don't struggle with burnout anymore and that I'm always more like Mary than Martha. But I can't. While I'm wiser about my limits, the need to recharge weekly, and the importance of nurturing my own soul, I still struggle with balancing the work of ministry with the work of God in my life.

04 Perfect Kids

Then little children were brought to Jesus for him to
place his hands on them and pray for them.
But the disciples rebuked those who brought them.
Jesus said, "Let the little children come to me,
and do not hinder them, for the kingdom of heaven
belongs to such as these."
— Matthew 19:13-14

I THOUGHT LOVING KIDS WAS ON THE SAME CONTINUUM AS liking them — that if I liked teenagers I would begin to naturally love them.

This belief was challenged when God sent Matt to my youth group. Matt had been raised in the church by parents who were highly involved in the life of the church. I liked Matt's parents, but I didn't like Matt. Matt never listened, purposely defied what I told him, and went out of his way to make my life miserable. He had the attitude that youth group existed only to serve his needs and he couldn't care less about what I thought. If he felt something was stupid or boring, he never hesitated to tell me.

I wasn't obvious about my feelings toward Matt, but my heart was closed toward him. On the outside I treated him as I would treat anyone else—I said all the right things. But on the inside, I found it hard to pray for him or desire God's best for his life. I kept telling myself that if Matt ever came around—if he ever became likable—I would be more than willing to invest my life into his. I would be more than willing to love him.

I'm embarrassed and sad to say that while I knew him, Matt never did "become likeable enough" for me to love him. God had yet to teach me the important difference between liking students and loving them.

God continued to bring more "Matts" into my ministry, and I became more and more frustrated with them. The story was the same for Mark, Molly, or John—for all of the kids who were rude, demanding, indifferent, and hard to get along with.

"Our youth group would be great if it weren't for so and so," I would say to myself. Instead of dealing with my inability to love certain teenagers, I put the blame and responsibility on them.

Frustrated with this experience, I sought the counsel of a veteran youth worker. His advice was "move with the movers and shake with the shakers." He told me not to waste my time with the apathetic and disrespectful kids but instead give my attention to the kids who were respectful and responsive. I took his advice—it was easy to follow. I ignored the unlikable students and focused on ones who seemed to care. For the most part, it seemed to work.

Instinctively—or maybe after being prompted by God—I began to realize this wasn't the right solution. I couldn't see Jesus acting this way toward hard-to-like teenagers. Jim Marian's book *Growing Up Christian* helped me see a small piece of the problem: I didn't understand the needs and issues of teenagers who had grown up in the church. Unlike me, the majority of my students couldn't remember a time when they weren't Christian—or when they weren't actively involved in the church. Because I kept relating my very different faith experience to theirs, I couldn't relate to them.

Growing up Christian, many of my students were struggling with issues I didn't understand—such as "excessive church syndrome"—an unofficial yet very real experience of being so overexposed to church that it loses its meaning. And other issues like guilt over not measuring up, unspoken spiritual doubts, and a wrong notion that going to church was somehow the same as loving Jesus. I knew my faith "firsthand"—I owned it when I chose to follow Christ as a teenager. But many of these students had a "secondhand faith." They were living off the faith of their parents, friends, and Christian teachers. After reading Jim's book, I began to see some of my hard-to-like students in a different light. Instead of being put off by their apathy and arrogance, I felt compassion for them and looked for ways to help them own their faith.

God gave me an opportunity to put this into practice with Marcus. Marcus had recently started coming to youth group from another church across town. From the first moment he came to our group, he expressed a bored, "I don't want to be here" demeanor. In the past, I would have challenged him to pay attention and take his faith more seriously. But this time, I took a different approach.

After church one Sunday I asked if we could talk. I told him I'd noticed he wasn't getting much out of youth group and that I was wondering if I could help. At first, he gave me familiar excuses, "I'm just tired from last night" or "I really *was* paying attention but you just couldn't tell." Instead of arguing with his reasons, I asked a simple question, "How long have you been going to church?" Without any hesitation, he shot back, "My whole life."

"Do you enjoy going to youth group or is this something you're forced to do?"

After a slight pause, he said, "I pretty much have to go whether I want to or not."

At this point, I could have said several things, most of which probably wouldn't have helped the situation. Instead, I asked him if I could talk to his parents about this. A little reluctant at first, he agreed. After talking with his mom, we determined that Marcus shouldn't be required to go to youth group, but only to the main service with the whole family.

I didn't see Marcus for a long time at a youth meeting or event, but I did continue to see him at the worship service almost every Sunday. Then one day he suddenly showed up at youth group again. He was a totally different person. Not only was he staying awake, he was opening himself up to new ideas—he was exploring his faith in a honest way along with the rest of the youth group. Over time, he became a much more involved student.

By taking the time to understand Marcus and his struggles—unique struggles of someone who had grown up in the church—God showed me how to connect and love him for who he was.

LOVING NON-CHRISTIAN TEENAGERS

My journey of learning to love teenagers wasn't limited to churched kids. I had to learn how to love unchurched, non-Christian teenagers, too. Unlike Christian kids who shared a common vocabulary and rarely asked the tough questions, unchurched teenagers often had no understanding of the Christian subculture and *every* question they asked was tough.

It didn't help that my youth group had very few non-Christian students and that almost none of my Christian students had any close non-Christian friends. And I didn't sense a lot of encouragement from the church leadership to reach out specifically to non-Christians. From the church, I heard a rather strong message that my primary job was to care for the Christian teenagers in the church. If I happened to reach non-Christian teenagers along the way, that was a nice bonus. But it was not vital.

This wasn't a problem for me at first—I only knew evangelism in the "high-pressure sales" context, and I didn't want to have anything to do with that. So instead of worrying about all the non-Christian students in my community, I focused all my energies discipling Christian kids.

Everything changed when God jogged in me a memory from early in ministry. I remembered my college pastor sharing at a staff meeting about his desire to develop a ministry to college students who rode the bus to campus every day. As he spoke, I responded outwardly with all the right words, "That's a great idea! It would be awesome if we figured out a way to reach more non-Christian students through a bus ministry!" Inwardly, I was thinking, "Who cares?"

As I revisited that memory, I realized I had been simply going through the motions of fulfilling the Great Commission.

Now, as I considered the non-Christian kids in my youth group, I was disturbed by that way of thinking. For the first time I faced the fact that I just didn't have a burden for non-Christian kids. So I prayed a simple prayer: "Lord, please give me a burden and desire to love non-Christian teenagers."

A funny thing started happening as a result of this prayer. I started noticing things I had never noticed before. When I would go to the mall or eat at Taco Bell or Carl's Jr, I couldn't help but pay attention to all the unchurched teenagers around me. I began to feel a growing affection toward them and a concern for their spiritual condition. Before I knew it, I was asking myself, "What can we do to reach all these non-Christian students?" God changed my heart toward non-Christian teens. And as my heart changed toward unchurched teens, God began to bring more non-Christians to our ministry.

The real test came when God brought a non-Christian student named Todd to our youth group. Within a short period of time, Todd gave his life to Christ. We started meeting regularly so I could help him get grounded in his new faith. Things were going well till we started talking about turning over various areas in his life to God. While he was generally open to identifying areas God might want him to surrender, there was one area he wasn't sure he wanted to give up. He liked smoking. Even though he was underage, Todd smoked a lot.

At first, I didn't make a big deal about it. But as the weeks went on, I started pressuring him to give up smoking as part of his new commitment to God. Rather than easing up when he hesitated, I pushed even harder, making a big deal about his need to quit smoking. For some reason, I couldn't let it go to focus on more important issues, and it became a dividing point between us. He started missing our meetings and eventually stopped coming to youth group.

While some might say that Todd's resistance to stop smoking was evidence that he was never truly committed to following Christ, I'll never know because I didn't know how to love him. I didn't know how to give him the space or the grace he needed to become the person God wants him to be. I regret that experience, but God used it to teach me an important lesson about what it means to love teenagers. Fortunately, God gave me another opportunity to put this lesson into practice.

LOVING HARD-TO-LIKE TEENAGERS

Chris was different from the majority of the teenagers in the youth group. His mom was a single parent who worked multiple jobs, he didn't have much money, he dressed differently from everyone else, and he carried himself like a tough guy. He frequently got into fights, was failing in school, and getting into trouble for drug use and other delinquent behavior. By the time he arrived in our youth group, he had run away several times, been in trouble with the police, and was in jeopardy of flunking the eighth grade, which he eventually did. As a result of coming to youth group, he made a decision to become a Christian. Despite his new faith in Christ, he was really struggling to live it out.

Everything came to a head one day when his mom called me because she was fed up with Chris. She had kicked him out of the house and was planning to send him to a group home. She was at her wit's end, reaching out in desperation. I didn't want Chris to go to a group home or see his relationship with his mom completely disintegrate, so I asked if Chris could stay at my house for a few weeks while everyone cooled off. Chris' mom agreed, and I picked him up later that day.

When Chris first arrived at my house, he was thankful for everything I was doing. I told him I wanted to see God redeem this situation and hopefully reunite him with his mom, who wasn't a Christian.

Chris was attending summer school to avoid having to repeat the eighth grade, and my youth intern and I took on the full-time job of getting him up in the morning, driving him to school, picking him up four hours later, bringing him back to church to help out, taking him home after work, and making sure he did his homework. After a couple of days of this exhausting routine, my intern (who was also staying with us) and I had a rather penitent conversation about how unappreciative we realized we'd been toward our parents when we were teenagers.

It didn't take long for Chris' disposition to change. Before you knew it, he was giving me attitude, lying to me, and just being a pain in the butt. I was tempted to yell at him, tell him how ungrateful he was, and threaten to kick him out of my house. But by God's grace, I resisted the urge and spent time praying through my emotions instead. God gave me a supernatural patience for Chris.

I didn't have the power to change Chris into the person God wanted him to be, but I discovered the power to love him like Jesus would. I wish I could tell you that my investment in Chris changed his life forever and that now he works for Billy Graham or is a youth pastor somewhere, but the truth is, the last time I spoke to Chris, he was still struggling to live out his faith. Did my time with Chris have any positive impact on him? I think so. I hope so. But without question, it had an impact on me.

I learned what it means to love tough teenagers. Maybe God waited so long to send someone like Chris to my ministry because I wasn't ready to love a student like him. I was ready now.

Before my time with Chris, I saw myself more as a talent scout than a good Samaritan. My job was to identify students who were responsive, eager to grow spiritually, and possessing leadership potential. As a talent scout, I lacked important qualities such as compassion, mercy, and patience. But when I began to see myself as a Good Samaritan, everything changed. I saw ministry through different eyes. No longer limiting myself to easy-to-work-with students, I felt called—compelled to love the unlovable, the hurting, angry, at-risk, and hard-to-reach students.

Jennifer was another hard-to-love teenager—but by no fault of her own. She had been sexually and physically abused by her parents and came to our youth group after moving in with her aunt and uncle. Jennifer was a deeply troubled young girl—she even attempted suicide while a member of our group. We didn't give up on her. Members of the youth group and I visited her every day while she was in the hospital. We stuck by her even though it was difficult. And we saw God work powerfully in her life. Her time with us was brief—she eventually ended up in a group home, no longer allowed to come to church. But what an amazing day of celebration when she returned to visit the youth group after being released from the group home at age eighteen! She had found in the youth group a safe place.

A place of love.

A place that wouldn't have felt of love at all had I not discovered this ability to love difficult teenagers. Learning to love kids was a God-given gift. A gift with many names.

Names like Chris. And Jennifer.

05 Perfect Parents

Hear, O Israel:
The LORD our God, the LORD is one.
Love the LORD your God with all your heart
and with all your soul and with all your strength.
These commandments that I give you today
are to be upon your hearts.
Impress them on your children.
Talk about them when you sit at home
and when you walk along the road,
when you lie down and when you get up.
Tie them as symbols on your hands
and bind them on your foreheads.
Write them on the doorframes of your houses
and on your gates.

— Deuteronomy 6:4-9

"ARE YOU AFRAID OF PARENTS?"

Now there's a question I wasn't expecting.

"Are you *afraid* of parents?"

"I don't think so. Why?"

"Because every time we need to communicate something to parents, you always ask me to do it for you," answered my seasoned volunteer. And with that answer, I realized that she was right. I *was* afraid of parents. Parents made me anxious, insecure, and generally uncomfortable.

Growing up in a family where fighting and arguing with each other was a common experience, I didn't have the best of relationships with my parents. After high school, I was ready to move away to college and put some distance between us. And even after things did improve between us, I was still figuring out how to relate to them as an adult and not as a child—how to view them as equals and not authority figures. This was all going on in my early twenties when I first started in youth ministry. And quite simply, because I still hadn't worked out all my developmental issues with my parents, I had a hard time relating to the parents of my youth group. Instead of seeing them as normal, everyday people, I saw them as grown-ups and authority figures. As a result, I tended to avoid parents or limit my interactions with them.

It didn't help that I had essentially no friends who were older adults. I'd spent nearly all of my high school and college years exclusively among peers. As a result, I wasn't prepared to work with parents when I became a youth pastor.

So when I started working in youth ministry, I tended to find volunteers who were around my age. Until I recruited Sue. Sue had both a son and a daughter in the youth group. To my surprise, she didn't volunteer so she could spy on her kids, but to help out in whatever way possible. As I got to know Sue and feel more comfortable around her, I began to relate better to the other parents as well. Sue played a key role in helping me to understand the needs and concerns of parents and how to relate to them.

In addition to being a wonderful volunteer, Sue and I developed a strong friendship. As Sue's son was approaching sixteen, she asked me for a favor. Sue and her husband, who were both working full-time, were finding it difficult to give Jerry the time he needed to prepare for his driver's license test. She asked if I would help teach him how to drive. I immediately said, "No problem." I drove an ambulance for four years; I was licensed to drive a motorcycle and a fifteen-passenger van. Clearly I was qualified for the job. I looked forward to the opportunity to pass on my excellent driving skills to Jerry.

I picked up Jerry from school for the first day of his driver training with his new vehicular sensei. I'm not quite sure what I was thinking—perhaps that my excellent driving skills would simply rub off because of proximity—but I didn't take him to an empty parking lot or a cemetery for his first lesson.

I just switched seats and said, "Let's go."

As soon as he hit the gas pedal, I started to panic. I began to wonder if he knew the differing purposes of the two pedals on the floor and if he'd had any experience playing racing video games and if that was a good or a very bad thing.

I reaffirmed my salvation as we barreled through town, missing cars left and right only by the grace of God. As we spurted and sped around town, I gripped my seat more tightly and my blood pressure rocketed. Somehow we survived without bodily injury or having to file any insurance claims. But as I drove home, I understood why parents don't want their children driving till they are thirty-five! Jerry did eventually learn to drive and passed his driving test with flying colors. A few years later, however, when he got into a big accident that totaled his car, I wondered if I'd shorted him a lesson or two.

PARENTAL SUPPORT

Long before I understood what it meant to support parents, I experienced what it meant to be supported by parents. Jack had been on the elder board for years, was currently the chairman, and was highly respected by others in the church. When I had first come to the church, I was apprehensive when I'd found out Jack's three children were all in the youth group. I worried about the potential negative consequences if I upset or ticked off one of his kids. In his wisdom, Jack sat me down from the start and told me he realized his children weren't saints and that if they ever stepped out of line, I shouldn't hesitate to discipline them. It was a breath of fresh air as I felt the freedom to do what was right instead of play church politics.

Jack's support shined the brightest during budget time one year. I had put together an aggressive youth budget so we could do more mission trips and outreach events. But after showing the proposed budget to my senior pastor, my excitement about building the youth ministry quickly faded. He told me it was unlikely the elder board would approve my budget as it was. He was preparing me for what he saw was an inevitable letdown. My budget would certainly be cut.

After all the important meetings were over, I waited to hear just how much money had been cut from my proposed budget. I was completely blown away when I found out that my budget had been approved exactly as I had proposed it. At first, I thought I had gotten incorrect information, but after confirming it a second time, I was happily in shock. One of the elders told me that Jack had gone to bat for me because of what he'd seen happen in the lives of his children. For the first time in my ministry career, I understood what it meant to experience the full support of a parent.

I experienced another level of parental support after I recruited a parent as a volunteer leader. We were having a difficult time finding someone who would teach junior high Sunday school (imagine that) until John finally offered to take on the challenge. Not only did the junior high students love John, but he also started going to many of the youth group special events, including our retreats. Shortly after a retreat, some parents had heard some disturbing rumors and were calling into question the safety and integrity of the weekend. Despite my explanation to parents about what had happened, many of them were not entirely convinced. Only after John took the time to explain what really went on were they finally convinced. John's support helped me to maintain the trust and confidence of several parents.

Years later at another church, I proposed changing the time of our high school Sunday school so it wouldn't compete with the morning worship services. Because we didn't have an adult Sunday school, parents would go to worship service while their children would go to Sunday school. I didn't see this as a problem for younger children, but I was troubled by the fact that junior high and especially high school students rarely attended services. I felt that if teenagers weren't a part of the main service, they would struggle to integrate into the larger church once they left the youth group. Knowing the sobering statistics for the number, or lack thereof, of students who transition from youth group to the larger church further strengthened my conviction.

My senior pastor supported this decision, but I knew that without parental support it wouldn't work. I knew there could be resistance to my idea since it might require more time investment from parents who often were the means of transportation for their kids. Instead of making the change and dealing with the backlash, I met with key parents to hear what they thought about my proposed change. Some of the parents were open to the idea, but others had their reservations. Yet even those with concerns were willing to support me because I had taken the time to tell them why I was considering this change and listen to their concerns. We did make the change, and there were a number of parents who struggled with it. But because of the support of key parents, we were able to make the move without significant backlash or opposition.

I wouldn't have survived as a youth pastor without the support of parents. Especially for junior high ministry, parental support is critical. Many junior high parents "freak out" about their children becoming full-blown teenagers and therefore have lots of questions and concerns about the youth program. If I didn't have their confidence and support, it would only be a matter of time before I lost their kids and an opportunity to influence them for Christ. It was only after I began to see parents as allies and not rivals that I was able to really put this into practice. We were on the same team. I needed them just as much as they needed me.

SUPPORTING PARENTS

It took me longer to understand the importance of supporting parents. Growing the youth group had always been more important to me than growing the family. It was only after an unchurched parent reached out to me that God brought this ministry mistake into focus.

Grace's mom was a single parent who worked long hours in order to provide for her family. She had a second child who was physically handicapped, adding to her burden and struggle. Even though she never went to church, she felt it was important for her children to go. Yet because of her work schedule and financial situation, she had difficulty driving her kids to church or affording our youth trips. She called me one day and shared that Grace really enjoyed church but wasn't going to be able to go anymore because of a change in her work schedule. I told her I would make sure Grace had a ride every Wednesday and she happily agreed.

My wife became Grace's weekly chauffeur and grew close to her during that time. Grace's faith began to take off as she involved herself in the group and she started bringing her non-Christian friends, many of whom later gave their lives to Christ. Eventually her older brother, Jared, started coming. Despite being physically handicapped, everyone embraced him because he was Grace's brother. I didn't see Grace's mom often, but her gratitude for the ways in which we supported her was evident.

A family crisis taught me just how important that support was. Grace's grandfather had been struggling with pancreatic cancer. Because both Grace and Jared were close to their grandfather, we talked about his condition as it worsened. When he died, it was very hard on Grace and Jared. I was surprised when Grace's mom asked me to do the funeral. I was the closest thing to a pastor they had. I was twenty-seven years old, I'd never done a funeral, and I didn't even own a black suit, so I was pretty nervous about the whole process. God was faithful as he helped me support their family and muddle my way through the service. After the funeral was over, Grace's mom thanked me again for all I'd done for her and her family. As I drove home that day, I couldn't help but thank her for allowing me to become a part of her family's support system. I never looked at parents the same way again. Parents needed my support as much as I needed theirs.

PARENT MINISTRY FAILURES

My attempts to support parents weren't always so positive or successful. Within a short period of time after coming to youth group, it became obvious that Robin was having lots of problems with her mom. One of the early clues was that Robin was having a hard time getting her mom to pick her up from youth group. Later, her small-group leader shared with me how Robin was struggling to get along with her mom. Everything came into focus the day Robin ran away from home. Her mom didn't know where to turn and eventually called me for help. We were able to find Robin relatively quickly and got her home safely. I recommended that we meet regularly for a while to talk through the issues in their relationship. Both Robin and her mom agreed.

At first, the meetings went well. With the incident fresh in everyone's mind, there was an openness to change. We talked about compromising on things, like how much time Robin could talk on the phone or spend with friends. We also discussed respect and kindness and how Robin needed to obey her mom and that her mom needed to be more gentle and supportive of her.

Just when I thought things were going well, they had another blowup. Robin didn't run away this time, but things had changed dramatically between them. Our meetings became more and more frustrating, and I wasn't sure how to break through. Robin's mom didn't want my help anymore. She had decided what the problem was and how she was going to handle it. Unfortunately, her interpretation of the problem didn't mesh with Robin's, and they continued to battle and fight.

I felt frustrated and defeated, and I didn't know what to do anymore. I developed a bad attitude toward Robin's mom when she decided that Robin could no longer come to youth group. Even though I continued to support Robin, I remained discouraged about the whole situation. Robin was able to come back eventually, but unfortunately, things with her mom continued to go back and forth with no visible progress. It was during times like these that I had to trust God to redeem the situation no matter how bleak things looked.

PARENTAL ADVICE

Thankfully, there were other times when my support role seemed to do some good. Steve's mom was the art teacher at our church's Christian school. She came to me for advice because of her frustration with Steve. Steve was a great kid, but he wasn't the most responsible teenager (Is that an oxymoron?). Because he attended the same school where his mom taught, she was his daily ride. Every morning she would wait for him to get ready for school. This entailed waking him once. Waking him again. Telling him to hurry up and get into the shower. Reminding him to "hurry up" as he labored to get ready for school. They rarely left on time, and she was often late for her own class. Frustrated by these experiences, she came to me for advice.

Because I'd just read the book *The Relaxed Parent* by Tim Smith, I had some borrowed wisdom to share. One of the key points of the book is that children become irresponsible because parents shield them from the consequences of their actions. Steve's mom had taken responsibility for waking him up and reminding him to get ready for school. And when Steve arrived late, she wrote him a note so that he wouldn't get a tardy or detention. Armed with my new insights on how to parent teenagers, I suggested she have Steve set his own alarm clock. And I suggested that she tell him when she was leaving and that if he wasn't in the car at that time, she'd leave without him.

I didn't think she would actually follow my advice. Though I had read a few books on parenting and certainly knew teenagers reasonably well, I was no expert. Usually, parents would listen politely, then do whatever they were already doing. I was shocked when, not long after our conversation, I saw Steve huffing and puffing up to school with his bike—twenty minutes after the tardy bell had rung.

He told me his mom had notified him that morning that if he didn't get ready in time, she was going to leave without him. He didn't believe her and had gone back to sleep. He woke up to the sound of the car leaving and freaked out. In a panic, he raced to get ready, hopped onto his bike and rode to school for the first time in years. Steve was sweating and catching his breath as he told me his story. I didn't have the heart to tell him that I might have been responsible for his predicament. Instead, I offered to carry his bike. For the rest of the day, I couldn't help but smile every time I saw Steve in the hallway.

WE ARE BETTER TOGETHER THAN WE ARE ALONE

This may not sound like profound wisdom, but I have learned that living with a teenager full-time is a lot harder than living with one for only a few hours a week. I get to see teenagers at their best. Parents don't have this luxury—they see their teenagers at their worst and can't send them "home" when they get obnoxious. Whether parents accept or reject my support, it should never stop me from reaching out and offering to help them in whatever way possible. Raising a teenager is not meant to be a one-person or even a two-person job, but rather should involve the extended family and the entire church. We need each other more than we realize. As a friend of mine would often say, "We are always better together than we are alone."

06 Perfect Coach

It was he who gave some to be apostles,
some to be prophets, some to be evangelists,
and some to be pastors and teachers, to prepare God's
people for works of service, so that the body of Christ
may be built up until we all reach unity in the faith and
in the knowledge of the Son of God and become mature,
attaining to the whole measure of the fullness of Christ.
— Ephesians 4:11-13

"GREAT ATHLETES RARELY MAKE GREAT COACHES" WAS A STATE-
ment that didn't make sense to me until I became a youth pastor.
I'd always assumed that if you were great at your sport or trade,
you would naturally make a great coach, one who could show
others how to be just as good. Turns out being great with teenagers
didn't necessarily mean I knew how to coach others to *work* with
teenagers.

It took me a while to figure this out. The first mistake I made
was thinking I could do ministry alone. Being the youth pastor, I
assumed it was my *job* to do the work of ministry. Everyone else

was to play the role of cheerleader. So they did—well, at least they watched with some level of implied support (and perhaps a growing morbid curiosity about how long I could last as a lone ranger)—while I enjoyed being a superhero youth worker, single-handedly reaching and loving teenagers.

But then I started to run into problems.

The first problem was a collision between my determination to lead worship and my near-complete lack of musical talent. Not only was I barely able to play guitar, but I couldn't sing on key if my life depended on it. In order to reflect my ability accurately, the Scripture reference in my Bible about "making a joyful noise to the Lord" has underlines and highlights and arrows pointing to that word "noise." After multiple attempts at trying to lead worship, we stopped having worship all together (to the relief of all who were lovers of music, I expect).

The second problem was a certain lack of creativity when it came to planning events. I struggled to come up with anything that was fun, interesting, or exciting, though, I did excel at an event known as "eating pizza and playing video games." What special events I could come up with I borrowed from youth ministry books. But they never seemed to work like they were supposed to.

And the third problem—which I shouldn't have seen as any great surprise since this is probably true for all male youth pastors—was my inability to minister effectively to the girls in the youth group. Because my wife wasn't able to help out regularly in the early years of ministry, I couldn't rely on her to be my adult female counterpart. I felt uncomfortable spending time with the girls outside of youth group unless it was with a larger group of students. With all the scandals that were happening in the news, I was pretty freaked out about being accused of something improper or inappropriate. To increase my paranoia, the youth pastor before me had been asked to leave due to inappropriate behaviors toward some girls. Of course, it didn't help that as a guy who was into computers, videos games, and playing sports, I felt out of touch with many of the girls' needs and what they were going through. Instead of looking for a solution to this problem, I just spent the majority of my time with guys and reasoned that the girls would understand. It didn't take long for the girls to feel ignored.

RECRUITING VOLUNTEERS

When I finally realized that I needed help—and lots of it—I thought people would come running to my aid. Isn't that how it's supposed to work? So I made an announcement in church seeking more volunteers. People smiled at me, told me what a good job I was doing, and said they would pray for me.

But none of them showed up to help.

I made a few more announcements. More smiles, more kind words, more prayers. And more no-shows.

I started asking people at random if they had ever considered working with teenagers. After being turned down multiple times, I developed a "rejection complex" and reduced my attempts at asking so I wouldn't feel that rejection again.

When I did approach people, I opened with this compelling

line: "I know you're probably too busy to volunteer, so I understand if you say no . . . " or this one: "You're probably not interested in working with teenagers, but just in case . . . " If I had approached dating the way I was approaching recruiting volunteers, I'd still be single. Fear of rejection made me wonder if recruiting volunteers was even worth the effort. I considered giving up and grabbing the superhero cape once again.

I did have some success recruiting high school students to work with my junior highers, though this had its own set of problems. For one thing, I failed to realize that I couldn't treat high school students the way I treated adults. I remember giving one of the high school students an evaluation of her performance as a volunteer. She broke out in tears. All she heard in my attempt to encourage and shape her skills was that I didn't like her and thought she was a failure. As a result, she stepped down as a volunteer.

Some of the high school students I recruited just weren't mature enough to lead other students. I knew I had a problem when I was disciplining my high school student leaders more often than I was my junior highers. Things really came into focus for me when, shortly after I left that church, I learned that one of the high school students I had recruited to work with the junior highers was pregnant. I hadn't taken the time to learn about her relationship with God or whether she was spiritually mature enough to work with students, and I made the mistake of setting her up to be a role model for others. I realized that recruiting high school students wasn't the best solution to my volunteer crisis. I was so desperate for help and tired of getting rejected that I failed to distinguish qualified and godly volunteers from unqualified and immature ones.

By not recruiting and training volunteers to be effective leaders, I did the entire church a disservice. Acting as a one-man show, I allowed the ministry to be completely dependent on my direction and presence. When I left that church, I left behind a leadership vacuum. The youth group struggled even more than before I had arrived. At first, I selfishly saw the failure of the youth group upon my departure as a sign of how much they had needed my leadership. But the more I reflected on this, the more I saw my failure as a leader. If Jesus has led his ministry this way, Christianity would have never survived.

EMPOWERING VOLUNTEERS

I was highly motivated to recruit a team of godly and committed volunteers at my next church. Instead of begging for help and taking anyone who showed interest, I kept my standards high as I shared my vision for impacting youth. I stopped worrying about rejection and started trusting that God was preparing the right people to become volunteer leaders. I worked closely with the senior pastor and elder board and put together a list of potential volunteers. Then I spent a long time in prayer about this before moving forward.

The good news was that I was successful at recruiting the right volunteer leaders. The bad news was that I wasn't sure what to do with them once I got them.

This hit home when I almost lost two of my best volunteers. Tim and Sarah were a married couple who both taught at a Christian school and loved working with teenagers. They were excited to come on board and couldn't wait to start helping. But that's where I blew it. Instead of taking the time to orient them to the ministry and to help them identify where they best fit, I assumed they would figure things out on their own. Week after week they came to youth group and stood around as I did my thing. Well, that's not quite true. They helped set up the room. They drove students places for me. But that was about it. They spent very little time one-on-one with the students.

After a few months of this, Tim called me.

"Sarah and I are thinking about stepping down as volunteers. Things have been really busy for us and it seems like you have everything under control."

The second I heard these words, I knew I had blown it. Even though Tim didn't say it directly, I knew that I had failed to help them develop a ministry that made them feel truly involved, truly needed. They felt useless and frustrated. I swallowed my pride and resorted to a familiar posture of begging, asking them to stay on a little bit longer so I could fix my mistake. Thankfully, they agreed. Over the next month, we spent time figuring out where they could use their gifts, passions, and experience to serve students. Once they found their areas of ministry, they went on to become great volunteers and remained on the youth staff for several years, even after I was no longer at that church.

Tim and Sarah volunteered because they wanted to effect

positive change in teens' lives. I was selling my volunteers short when I assumed that they just wanted to help with the mundane ministry tasks.

I still had much to learn about working with volunteers. I had unrealistic expectations of how much time volunteers needed to give. Because I didn't have all the volunteers I needed, I expected too much from the ones I did have. When you're a full-time minister, you don't always have a grasp of how your volunteers are balancing work, family, and friends with their church roles. Far too often I laid a guilt trip on volunteers if they had to miss a special event. I even spiritualized my reasoning by saying things like, "Jesus would want you to go to the all-nighter," or "If we don't have enough adults for summer camp, it will ruin the camp for everyone." Being insensitive to their needs and out of touch with their other commitments, I pushed my volunteers toward burnout.

The hard reality was one you probably know all too well—you can't have enough volunteers. Challenged once again by my arrogance and ignorance, I realized my error and began making changes. I stopped asking them to show up to every event and every meeting and asked them to commit to only Sundays or Wednesdays. And the only special events I wanted every volunteer to attend were our camps and retreats.

The other change I made was how I planned special events. The way I used to do things was to work out every detail of an event, then ask volunteers to help implement my plan. When the volunteers had no input on when an event would happen or what kind of event we would do, they held little ownership of it. So when I asked them to show up and support a youth event, few were interested. But when I started involving volunteers at all levels of planning, everything changed. As volunteers shared their ideas, took responsibility for different parts of the events, and picked dates that worked for everyone involved, their interest and commitment to participate skyrocketed. Not only did more volunteers start showing up at special events, they practically ran the events all by themselves. We wouldn't even host an event unless we had enough interest and availability from volunteers.

CONTINUAL STRUGGLES

I still struggle with knowing how to best recruit and coach leaders. I've learned it's a constant learning process. At one church, I got so frustrated with trying to recruit leaders that I gave up trying. For about a year. I joked that since the average age in the church was sixty-five, nobody wanted to work with youth because they were afraid of having a heart attack or suffering a stroke. Despite my previous recruiting success, I developed that familiar rejection complex. It was only after God supernaturally sent a few volunteers that I realized he was still working even though I had given up. Slowly but surely, God began to bring more volunteers into the ministry. One of these new volunteers turned out to be the best worship leader I'd ever had.

I've often struggled with balancing my time between volunteers and students. I've often felt guilty because I didn't spend enough time with adult leaders. I used to rationalize that adult volunteers didn't need my attention; after all, they were *adults*. I also thought it was the senior pastor's job to care for my volunteers. I've since realized that volunteers need my attention and leadership just as much as my students do.

When I've failed them, the ministry has suffered. One volunteer was struggling to relate to teenagers, so she came to me for help. Instead of taking the time to work with her and listen to her struggles, I handed her a few books and assumed she would find her way to the answers that were obviously contained in those hallowed pages. Unfortunately, she never did. She stepped down before even finishing a year. It broke my heart when I realized that I'd lost a great volunteer because of my failure to give her the time and attention she deserved.

There's another kind of volunteer I haven't yet talked about: the inherited volunteer. You know these well if you've recently started your ministry. These are the people who have always worked with the youth group — or at least it seems that way since you're the "new kid." Inherited volunteers have a history with the youth ministry, and they don't always welcome change. But they also bring perspective and experience that a youth pastor can't know in the first months of a new ministry position.

I didn't see that benefit at first, and waved "good-bye" to a number of inherited volunteers who didn't match the vision I believed was more important than the experience they brought to the table. I realize now that many of them left simply because I changed things too fast and didn't show them the respect and value they deserved. Inherited volunteers deserve time and compassion. That doesn't mean caving into demands, but it does mean listening.

Despite my many failures in working with volunteers, I've had the privilege of serving alongside some of the best. There's nothing more exciting than seeing God touch the life of a student through the actions of a caring and committed volunteer. In many ways, I learned more about the nature of authentic ministry from my volunteers than I learned from anyone else.

The longer I'm in ministry, the more prone I am to forgetting why I work with teenagers, but my volunteers always bring me back to reality. Every time I see volunteers willingly and selflessly giving themselves to students, I'm reminded of the incredible impact God can make when an adult takes the risk of stepping into a teenager's world and loving them as Christ would. Volunteers are also great reminders that ministry isn't about recognition, career, or money, but about allowing God to use us to change lives. And, volunteers remind me that I should be thankful; I have the privilege of doing what they do . . . and I get paid for it, too.

07 Perfect Size

His master replied, "Well done, good and faithful servant!
You have been faithful with a few things;
I will put you in charge of many things.
Come and share your master's happiness!"
— Matthew 25:21

I WANTED A BIG YOUTH GROUP.

A really big group. The size other youth workers would marvel at.

I feel unspiritual admitting this, but the truth is, there were many times I focused more on the growth of the youth group than on the growth of the individual students. Of course when communicating with others, I disguised my real intentions by emphasizing that we needed to "reach more students for Christ" and that "God doesn't want our youth group to be a Christian club, but a lifesaving station." Sure, these were valid truths. But mostly, I wanted a big youth group.

My first Six Flags Magic Mountain trip was an early attempt to grow a bigger youth group. Students were supposed to bring their friends in droves, causing our youth group to double, maybe even triple in size. I spent countless hours on a sure-fire flier and then pushed, demanded, and begged students to bring their friends. On the night of the big event, I carefully organized the youth room, putting out twice the number of chairs we usually needed. I made full-size posters of the fliers and put them on the walls to build excitement about the event. I printed dozens of visitor cards so we wouldn't run out. I carefully taped prizes underneath every chair so I could surprise and woo students with my creativity and ingenuity.

I could hardly contain my excitement as students started to arrive.

And then I waited. The regulars showed up right on time.

So I waited some more.

Finally, after waiting far too long, I had to face the reality that there weren't going to be any visitors that night. My excitement morphed into disappointment and then into "unrighteous" anger toward my students. I grilled them about why they didn't bring their friends and called into question their spiritual commitment. Let's just say it wasn't a positive experience for anyone involved.

SIZE DIDN'T ALWAYS MATTER

I didn't always want a big youth group. When I first started in youth ministry, I was just excited to be working with kids, no matter how many or how few. I had just finished my internship working with a large college group where I wasn't able to know everyone, so I treasured the opportunity to spend significant time with a smaller number of students.

Before starting at one church, I asked for a photo of the youth group so I could learn everyone's name. It was an exciting first day when I was able to recite back all the names of the students and share with them my desire to invest in them and help them grow spiritually. Hanging out with students, getting to know their dreams and hurts, and being able to personally respond to them was a wonderful experience.

Over time, however, my motivations and desires began to change. Part of the change was "caught" from the people I began to look up to as youth ministry role models. All the youth workers who wrote books and taught others how to do youth ministry had large youth groups. I looked up to them as the obvious role models. I savored their familiar stories describing how when they first got to their churches there were only a handful of students, but amazingly and often dramatically God transformed their youth groups until they numbered in the hundreds. I wanted to be a part of something exciting and bigger than life—I wanted to see the same thing happen with my youth group.

How many times have you heard this question: "How big is your youth group?" That was usually the first question other youth workers would ask me, and it was another reason for the shift in my motives. After going to a few youth worker conventions and being asked this question again and again, I began to feel insecure about the size of my youth group. I started to answer this question by giving the most favorable number I could think of—which always was the attendance from our largest ever youth event plus a few extra students just in case I missed some. I began to pick up the message that the size of my youth group determined my importance as a youth worker. I even questioned my effectiveness as a youth worker because I didn't have a big youth group.

The final influencer on my changing motive came from my experience with church leaders. Whether I was having to report my weekly attendance, offer updates to the elder board, or type up my annual church report, I was reminded of the importance of numbers. It wasn't that the leadership didn't care about whether students were growing spiritually, but numbers were a convenient and tangible way to measure my effectiveness. It was a lot easier and more impressive to say that the youth group doubled in size than it was to explain the various ways students were growing in their faith.

To compound matters, I experienced the most praise for numerical growth. People offered all kinds of virtual (and literal) pats on the back for a job well done when the youth group was growing. After an especially well-attended outreach event, my senior pastor and I had this brief, yet telling conversation.

"How many students were at the all-nighter?" he asked.

"Around 120."

As I spoke the number out loud, I saw excitement and amazement in his eyes. I was certainly proud of the growth in numbers, and my pastor's affirmation made me feel good about myself and the youth ministry. I realize now that it was experiences like this that fed my hungry ego, confirming that I was a competent and professional youth worker. Surely a large youth group was the ultimate proof of this.

ADDICTED TO GROWTH

And so it began—the quest for an ever bigger youth group. I looked to the existing students for my first attempts to grow in number.

"Invite your friends to youth group, it will be fun." I probably said that a hundred times.

"I want everyone to think of at least one friend they want to invite next week." That one, too.

"Why don't any of you invite your friends to church?" I said that one when the first two didn't seem to get any results.

After repeated appeals, reminders, and exhortations, students still weren't inviting their friends. I became frustrated. I took out that frustration on students—making them feel guilty for not inviting friends. I found myself favoring those students who invited friends by paying more attention to them.

Somehow, I had missed the big picture. Just asking students to invite friends wasn't cutting it. Teenagers are often pretty intuitive—they knew my motives were wrong and didn't feel compelled to invite friends just to satisfy my "numbers" greed. Students needed a good reason to invite friends—I had failed to give them a vision for the Great Commandment and the Great Commission because of my improper motives.

I wasn't doing a very good job supporting the students' families during this numbers game time, either. Instead, I became irritated when parents allowed their kids to miss youth group because of homework or sports. I even reasoned myself into a corner of frustration, thinking thoughts like *God is more important than homework* and *Church should take priority over sports.* I never vocalized these feelings to parents, but I thought about them a lot and that impacted how I dealt with parents. Call it subtle manipulation, if you like, but I made a big deal to parents about the importance of youth group and how getting their kids involved in the youth group was one of the best things they could do. My real motive was to get more parents to bring their kids—thus, a bigger group.

But it didn't work. So I stopped pushing and demanding kids to invite their friends and focused my energies designing an attractive and exciting program that would magnetically draw students to church. I asked students, "What would it take for your friends to want to come to church?" I began to make changes in how we did youth group. We redecorated the room, bought an air hockey and foosball table, chose better music to add to the ambiance, played better games, and gave away lots of pizza. It worked. More students started inviting their friends.

I didn't stop there. I put more and more energy into creating an exciting and magnetic environment. And I searched the minds of the experts—my youth group kids—to find the next idea that would grow attendance. A laser tag all-nighter was one of their best ideas and it was a huge success. Growth was indeed happening, sometimes at an alarming rate.

One of the greatest challenges was maintaining the growth. I worried constantly about attendance. If we had an especially low turnout on a given night, too much of my attention was taken by that fact, and I gave less of myself to the students who were there. When attendance had sagged for a few weeks in a row, I sent out letters to the students who had stopped coming. Many of the students responded to the letters and started coming back, but it didn't always work. So I called students, persuading and even begging them to come back to youth group.

I've since realized that there is a normal ebb and flow to youth group attendance throughout the year. But at the time, I felt a constant pressure to maintain an upward slope on the growth chart. One summer I tried to boost our attendance by hosting a youth event *every day* of the summer. We had special events on Mondays, volleyball on Tuesdays, junior high group on Wednesdays, high school group on Thursdays, bowling on Fridays, beach days on Saturdays, and church on Sundays. I had it covered. I was proud of the frenzy of events I had put together; I was sure it would give me a bigger group. But the only thing it did was give me a nervous breakdown while practically burning out all my volunteers. It would have been much wiser for me to consider the summer as a time to enjoy the students who did come and deepen relationships with those kids.

AND EVEN BIGGER

The desire for a bigger group became somewhat of an addiction. After going to a seminar on how to promote your youth ministry,

I spent countless hours designing fliers, calendars, and other publicity attention-getters. I was greatly disappointed when I discovered that most of the kids weren't impressed or influenced by flashy publicity gimmicks, so I just kept on searching for the idea that *would* work. Meanwhile things like missions, student leadership, and worship faded into the background.

I began to see the success of my ministry relying more on what I did than on what God did. I tried to force things rather than wait on God's timing. While our junior high group was growing by leaps and bounds, the high school group had yet to experience significant numerical growth. Instead of seeing this as an opportunity to deepen the high school group and develop a core of student leaders, I tried forcing growth through big events and lots of hype.

"Don't you know the importance of visitors? We can't run out of these cards!" You know your addiction to growth is out of control when you yell at your staff for running out of visitor cards—you know, those information cards you collect on new people. Yeah, I did that. As you can imagine, my staff looked at me like I was a raving lunatic. I later apologized for my irrational outburst.

Attendance milestones are a funny thing. For some reason we love milestones and can't wait to reach the next one. At one church, I remember how excited I was when our junior high youth group broke twelve students on a regular basis. Twelve seemed like a particularly spiritual number, and it was far better than the previous average of five to six students per week. The feeling didn't last long. There were other milestones to reach.

My next church was relatively new and had struggled to get their youth ministry off the ground. I began with a handful of students. Within three months, however, we'd quadrupled in size and continued to grow steadily over the next year and a half. Once we hit the century mark — more than one hundred students — I should have been thrilled. I suppose I was . . . for a moment. But I wasn't satisfied. I began to think about how we could break two hundred.

More growth didn't satisfy; it just created a greater hunger for more growth. And as long as the youth group was growing, I didn't have to deal with my addiction. Recognition and praise for bigger numbers merely fueled the hunger. No one ever questioned my methods for creating growth or the motives behind the growth. My insecurities about sharing the size of my youth group with others disappeared with my numbers-success and suddenly I was more than happy to tell others about it. *Proud*, even. (Now there's a flashing yellow warning sign if there ever was one.) While on the surface I always gave God the glory for our growth, in my heart I took a lot of that credit — after all, it was the result of my hard work and ingenuity.

IN DENIAL

Like an alcoholic, I was in denial about my addiction and refused to see it for what it was. I was in denial about my role versus God's role in producing numerical growth. I had completely reversed the parable of the talents in Matthew 25, where Jesus reminds us that our role is to be faithful and God's role is to grant success. Instead of waiting for Jesus to say, "Well done, good and *faithful* servant," I was waiting for him to say, "Well done, good and *successful* servant." I had failed to realize that biblical growth is more about what God does than what I do.

I saw growth as a "high" I needed in order to feel good about myself and the ministry. When the numbers were up, I was up. But when the numbers were down, I was down. Like a yo-yo, my self-esteem fluctuated from week to week. I believe God wanted the youth group to grow, but he wanted me to depend on his power and wisdom, not on the growth itself.

Most important, I was in denial about my understanding of failure in ministry. I thought that failure needed to be avoided at all cost and I saw a small youth group as a sign of failure. It wasn't until I was nearly crushed by failure that I was able break free from my addiction to growth.

08 Perfect Success

We are your servants, the people you rescued by your
great power and might. O Lord, please hear my prayer!
Listen to the prayers of those of us who delight in
honoring you. Please grant me success now as
I go to ask the king for a great favor.
Put it into his heart to be kind to me.

— Nehemiah 1:10-11, *NLT*

FOR MOST OF MY LIFE, I'VE BEEN AFRAID. WHEN I WAS A BABY, I WAS afraid of strangers. When I was a child, I was afraid of the dark. When I was in elementary school, I was afraid of girls. When I was in junior high, I was afraid of never having a girlfriend. When I was in high school, I was afraid of not getting *into* college. And when I was in college, I was afraid of not getting *out* of college. Instead of my fear going away, it only changed forms.

The fear that has stayed with me longest is my fear of failure.

Growing up in an Asian family, success was more valued than happiness. Working hard and applying yourself were more important than feeling happy and fulfilled. This truth I lived was later confirmed when I was in college and learned about a study of Asian and Caucasian moms who were asked what their most important goal was for their children. Asian moms answered, "I want my children to be successful" and the Caucasian moms answered, "I want my children to be happy." Well, my parents were definitely in the "be successful" category. After all, that's how they made it to the United States. Both my parents came from poor families in mainland China and overcame their poverty by excelling in school and graduating with advanced degrees from prestigious universities in the United States. My dad eventually became a college professor and my mom an electrical engineer. My older brother did well to follow in their footsteps and today is practicing law with degrees in law, journalism, and biochemistry.

Mine was a different story.

I struggled with school. Though I excelled at math in my early years, by the time I got to high school, I had lost all interest.

"Why do I have to learn this? Who uses the quadratic equation anyway?"

It wasn't that school was difficult. I just wasn't interested.

In elementary school I earned more S's for satisfactory on my report card than O's for outstanding, much to the disappointment of my parents. I wanted to focus on martial arts, sports, and girls (and was relatively successful at the first two). With such a prime focus on grades, my parents didn't have much affirmation or approval left for extracurricular activities.

When I got to high school, grades mattered even more because suddenly they were the determining factor for the *rest of my life*—well, okay, for the kind of college I could attend. When I graduated in the middle of my class, I felt like a failure, particularly because many of my friends were graduating at the top. I almost didn't get into a four-year college, and when I did, I brought along an inferiority complex. Despite having excelled at sports and recently become a Christian, failure was a familiar friend. I tried to appear confident and together, but on the inside, I was insecure and unsure of myself.

MINISTRY AND FAILURE

I brought these failure issues with me into youth ministry. I held tightly to the belief that if I were a competent youth worker, I would never be seen as a failure. If I developed my skills as a youth worker, they would *protect* me from failure.

My search for competency led to an obsession with seminars and books; I became a "seminar-aholic." I went to seminars on creative teaching, crisis counseling, theology and youth culture, student leadership, creating a youth budget, and women in youth ministry. I went looking for the tools and skills I needed to be a competent youth worker—a youth worker who would not know failure. I bought tons of tapes so I could listen to seminars I'd missed or review seminars I'd attended.

I read everything and anything I could find on youth ministry. I was constantly on the lookout for the latest and greatest youth ministry books. My wife joked that I should buy stock in CBD (Christian Book Distributors) because I was buying so many books from them. My library of youth ministry books grew exponentially.

And my competence grew, too. I became skilled in teaching, programming, leading volunteers, relational ministry, outreach, and every other category listed in the table of contents of youth ministry books and seminar brochures. My strategy was working: Instead of experiencing failure, I was being affirmed by church leaders, volunteers, students, and other youth workers. My compulsion to succeed increased even more when I started to receive affirmation as a speaker and an author. Becoming more competent didn't make my cravings lessen; it only strengthened my dependence.

CONTROLLING FAILURE

Failure, to me, was anything short of perfection. I didn't feel content even when things *did* go right. Failure was only one event, camp, or youth group away. If students started bringing lots of friends to youth group, I worried about friendships breaking up causing students to stop coming. If an outreach event was successful at reaching a large number of visitors, I worried about whether the visitors would make the transition to youth group. If attendance numbers were up, I worried about them crashing down.

My fear of failure made me reluctant to try anything new. I became obsessed with discovering what was *working* in other ministries instead of finding out what God wanted to do in our ministry. To make sure that something would not fail, I did everything humanly possible to make it happen. Afraid that not enough students were signing up for camp, I spent hours on the phone calling every student and encouraging, persuading, and even begging them to go.

It was rare for me to take risks, which, unfortunately, stunted innovation and creativity in my ministry. If someone came up with a new idea and I wasn't sure if it would succeed, I discouraged it. One intern shared his idea of starting a skate ministry at the church and because I didn't think the church would go for it, I killed the idea. I carefully explained all the reasons for my decision — describing the obstacles and problems we would run into and why his idea wouldn't work. Could it have worked? Maybe. I'll never know. I just knew I didn't want to fail. And I wouldn't.

Everything was about to change at my next church.

ENCOUNTERING FAILURE

Just over a dozen students showed up at my first Wednesday night meeting. That would be a fine number for many churches, but twenty years before, this youth ministry was reaching over six hundred high school students a week. Okay, deep breath. There would be many challenges ahead — but I was confident I could quickly turn the ministry around. Things certainly couldn't get any worse.

Seven months later we hit an all-time low of eight students. *Eight.*

I kept thinking more students were going to show up. "They must just be running late." Those fateful eight peppered me with questions that weren't helping my confidence, including, "Where is everybody?" and the rather demoralizing, "Did we cancel youth group tonight?" I even went outside a few times just to make sure nobody was lost. There were no stragglers.

Squeezing the students onto two couches, the room looked enormous that night. The game I planned wouldn't work with such a small group so I improvised and came up with a stupid game everyone hated. I lethargically struggled through my lesson, offering the somewhat ironic analogy that as God used Nehemiah to rebuild the walls of Jerusalem for his glory, he wanted to use us to rebuild the youth group for his glory. I had a hard time believing my own lesson. How could I expect my students to believe it?

I went home depressed.

Talk about bad timing—this low point happened just prior to the birth of my son. The very next week I was scheduled to take time off. I did, but I couldn't stop obsessing over the state of the youth group. I hoped and prayed things would improve when I returned. They didn't.

Five students.

I drove home that night crushed and demoralized, questioning why I was in youth ministry and what God was thinking when he led me to this church.

My grandiose idea of transforming the ministry overnight vanished. Nothing I tried was working. I put in longer days and worked harder than I ever had trying to grow the youth group. A year after starting at the church, the youth group wasn't any healthier or larger.

For the first time in ministry, I felt totally helpless and incompetent. I didn't know which was worse: knowing I had all the right skills but feeling helpless or realizing that my skills didn't mean anything. Though no one in leadership expressed serious concern, for the first time I had a genuine fear of being fired.

I also began to think about quitting. If I couldn't turn around the youth group, I didn't deserve to be the youth pastor. After all, they'd hired me so I could *help* the youth group, not hurt it. I wanted relief from my situation. I wanted to be put out of my misery.

I hit a wall of frustration, confusion, and self-doubt. Like David in the Psalms, I began to cry out to God in desperation.

I wanted to talk to my youth ministry friends about my struggles, but I was afraid they wouldn't understand. I tried to ease into the topic with a youth worker friend by asking how things were going in his youth group. He went on to share about all the exciting things happening and how God was blessing his ministry and how he was doing so well the church was going to double his salary. Okay, not all of that was true. But when his accolade and success-infused monologue was over, the last thing I wanted to do was share about my situation. I didn't want my friends to know how much I was struggling with self-doubt and fear. I was supposed to be a megachurch youth pastor—the one with all the answers. So I struggled alone.

In my solitude and discouragement, God slowly and painfully forced me to confront my fear of failure. God spoke powerfully through failure.

FROM FAILURE TO FAITH

The first thing God helped me see was that failure didn't destroy me. People didn't point fingers at me, the church didn't fire me, and God still loved me. Suddenly, failure didn't have the power over me it once did. Like a rite of passage, my battle with failure made me stronger, not weaker. After this experience, I could identify with what Lance Armstrong, seven-time Tour de France winner and cancer survivor, had to say in his book *It's Not About the Bike:*

> *The truth is, if you asked me to choose between winning the*
> *Tour de France and cancer, I would choose cancer . . . Odd*
> *as it sounds, I would rather have the title cancer survivor*
> *than winner of the Tour, because of what it has done for me*
> *as a human being, a man, a husband, a son, and a father.*[3]

While I wouldn't dare compare my experience to surviving cancer, I still felt like I understood where Armstrong was coming from. Avoiding failure through achievements and accomplishments had had its rewards, but it wasn't until I was overwhelmed with failure that I really grew as a Christian, leader, and pastor. I shared this experience with Dan Webster, a mentor of mine, and he replied, "Success doesn't teach a person anything after age thirty-five." His point was that success can only teach us so much; it's through the fiery furnace of failure that we truly learn and grow.

It may be no surprise to you that success and failure are not mutually exclusive, but it was to me. I assumed that failure and success couldn't coexist. You were either a failure or a success, a winner or a loser, competent or incompetent. If I didn't get all A's on my report card, I was a failure. If I didn't start every game or score the most points, I was a failure. If I didn't succeed in every aspect of my ministry, I was a failure.

Richard Farson and Ralph Keyes, in their book *Whoever Makes the Most Mistakes Wins*, helped me to change this kind of thinking:

> *Sometimes, what seems to be success at one point proves to be a failure at another. . . . We like to think you either succeed or fail. Most situations are more ambiguous, however. . . . Failure begets success followed by failure and success once again. . . . Under close scrutiny, failure and success are hard to distinguish. They are like fraternal, if not identical twins.*[4]

Failure pushed me forward. Some of my most innovative and creative ideas in ministry came after this realization. No longer bound by a fear of failure and suddenly free to take risks, ministry took on whole new dimensions.

Overcoming failure wasn't about having an absence of fear, but rather having the courage to act in spite of fear. Fear wasn't my enemy, but how I allowed fear to influence my life and ministry was. I learned to put my fear of failure in perspective and to manage and even harness my fear for God's purposes. And I trained my thinking from seeing failure as "an end to something" to seeing it as a new beginning.

09 Perfect Power

But he said to me, "My grace is sufficient for you,
for my power is made perfect in weakness."
Therefore I will boast all the more gladly about my
weaknesses, so that Christ's power may rest on me.
— 2 Corinthians 12:9

TRY HARDER!!!

This was my life philosophy. I lived by it in school, sports, and even in my family. I applied the same kind of thinking to ministry. It worked . . . for a time. For the first ten years of my ministry, I saw the direct connection between hard work and success.

Nobody warned me that there was a problem with this philosophy.

The first inkling I got that something was wrong was prompted by the book *Fresh Wind, Fresh Fire* by Jim Cymbala. In this book, Cymbala tells the story of how God used him as a young, inexperienced pastor in a small, struggling church to become a beacon of light for thousands of hurting people throughout Brooklyn, New York. Because of his dependence on God's power through prayer and surrender, God supernaturally transformed his church into a source of healing and strength for countless people. I know that book inspired many people to a deeper prayer life. But I came away with a deep conviction that I was going about leading my ministry in the wrong way. This conviction haunted me, even though my current youth ministry was experiencing amazing growth. I had a gnawing sense that I had developed the ministry more through my hard work and ingenuity than through God's power.

I didn't know who to talk to about this. It wasn't exactly the kind of topic I would want to bring up in casual conversation: "By the way, I think the success of my ministry is more a result of my personal drive than God's supernatural power. What do you think?" It definitely wasn't something I wanted to share with my senior pastor or bring up at the next staff meeting. And as I thought through all the seminars and books I had come across over the years, I was hard pressed to remember anyone admitting that they were guilty of building a thriving ministry on their own hard work and resourcefulness without depending on God.

As my conviction grew, it turned into a hunger for being in a place where I was forced to depend on God's power and strength for ministry. With a goal of deepening my dependence on God, I took some time off. I didn't know exactly what I was going to do, but I knew I needed the space to think. And besides that, I was tired and close to burnout.

The most meaningful experience during that time off was spent at a monastery in the company of monks. There I found a place and time to think and pray. This was a dramatic change of pace from my normal frenzied routine, and in the quiet I realized that I had substituted action and effort for prayer and dependence. Instead of learning to wait and depend on God for results, I had attempted to achieve results through my own power. While the results I achieved in this way may have seemed impressive to some, they were nothing compared to what God could do through my ministry.

As God revealed this to me, I yearned to lead a ministry where only the supernatural could explain the results. I didn't want to be in a ministry where I could explain all my success as the result of my effort and hard work anymore. I prayed that God would show me how to lead a ministry with complete dependence on him.

Before my time off, I had been thinking of moving on and exploring opportunities at other churches. But after my time off, I knew that decision was based more on burnout than God's leading. Even though I hadn't yet learned what it meant to fully depend on God, I did have a greater sense of peace about my ministry. I resolved to faithfully serve at my church until God made it clear that it was time to move on.

Three months later I received a call from another church. While I didn't know much about this church, I felt God wanted me to take some time to discern his will. I spent a month praying and seeking the counsel of others before finally meeting with one of the pastors on the search committee. After learning more about the youth ministry and having my questions answered, I took the next step and applied for the position. Another month passed.

I went through the interview process and was offered the job. I was confident I'd experienced confirmation throughout the entire process: from my wife, from my closest friends, from within, and from my current senior pastor. I knew God was leading me to accept this new challenge. And so, with high expectations, I accepted the position, convinced that God wanted to do great things in my next ministry.

A PRAYER OF SURRENDER

Remember that church where I experienced the most failure in ministry? This was it. For the first time in my career, I was stuck. After struggling for nearly two years with failure after failure, I reached a point of desperation. God was beating me over the head with failure, forcing me to let go of confidence in my abilities and experience. But it was like trying to pry a pit bull from his victim. I finally prayed, "God, I surrender. I admit I don't know what I'm doing, and it's only by your power that anything positive will happen in my ministry."

It was a prayer that I would have to pray many times.

I had been leading my ministry by sight and not by faith. I had put my trust in my abilities, skills, and experience. It was only after experiencing complete helplessness that I was forced to depend on God.

Right about this time, God reminded me of my earlier prayer in the monastery for him to teach me what it meant to fully depend on him. I laughed to myself and thought, "If I'd known God's answer to my prayer would involve so much pain and failure, I would have taken back my request." It reminded me of the old saying, "Be careful what you pray for because you might get it." Thankfully, God hadn't let me know ahead of time how he was going to teach me about surrender.

And he was only just getting started.

THE POWER OF GOD

A few months later, an interesting thing happened. Two students who had stopped coming to youth group a year before suddenly showed up. They had stopped coming because our ministry wasn't connecting with urban students. And even though urban students represented a large part of the community surrounding our church, what few we had when I first arrived had left long ago. With my prayer of surrender, my heart had been broken by the truth that I had no idea how to reach urban teens. I needed God's help. Their return was a sign of answered prayer. I asked God to show me how to love and connect with these urban guys. By God's grace, I was able to love them in a way that I hadn't been able to before. They began coming regularly and started bringing their friends. It was an exciting sight to see!

A few weeks later, another urban student who had stopped coming to youth group decided to return. In the past she would complain about how serious everything was, disrespect the rules and other people, and comment regularly on how she liked the previous youth pastor better than me. I had to constantly discipline her and sometimes even asked her to leave. As you might imagine, I was glad when she'd stopped coming.

However, the night she came back, things were different. Instead of seeing her as trouble, I felt a supernatural love toward her. Things weren't that different in her behavior, though — she ended up getting into a fight that I had to break up. I spent hours calling everyone involved to resolve things. In the past, I would have been really hard on her and would have told her that she wasn't welcome at youth group until she changed her behavior. But because God had changed my heart, I felt led to tell her that I was sorry we had had so many problems in the past and that I wanted to see God do something great in her life.

God transformed her heart and she began to open up. She shared her desire to get right with God and wanted to start coming to youth group for the right reasons. I couldn't believe what I was hearing. I kept thinking: *Is this the same student who terrorized my life when I first came to this church? Am I talking to the wrong person? Am I imagining this entire experience?* God once again demonstrated his power. After I talked to her about the consequences of her getting into a fight, I spent a long time listening to her share about her struggles. And I prayed with her. After I hung up the phone, I could barely believe what had just happened. Each week I would see her at youth group I was reminded of God's incredible power.

With increased success in reaching urban students, I wondered what I could do to improve. I asked God for guidance in this and he led me to an African-American youth worker friend. He told me that his kids were really into "Rap Battles" — where students would test their rap skills against each other in a lively, fun competition. As I listened, negative thoughts began to flood my mind, *It will never work, no one will show up. The suburban kids will freak out and stop coming to youth group. What am I thinking — I'm Chinese.*

But I couldn't let go of the idea, so I pitched it to the volunteers at our next meeting. They said, "Let's go for it!" Within a few weeks, we had picked a date and named the event, "Urban Underground." I asked the friend who gave me the idea if he would be willing to speak at the event since he'd been a Christian rap artist in his younger years. He agreed to come. Yet as the date grew closer, my anxiety rose.

When the night finally arrived, I couldn't believe what I saw. Right before my eyes, we were becoming a healthy and vibrant multicultural and multiethnic youth group. Not only did the usual students show up but a lot of urban students brought their friends and their friends' friends. It didn't matter that the rap battle fell through or that my pathetic attempts at rapping were met with laughter and amusement—the students had a great time and were *glad* they brought their friends. God made everything come together. I learned a simple truth that night—when I depend on God, anything is possible. Even if that means a suburban-raised Chinese youth pastor planning an urban outreach event in a suburban church where the average age is sixty-five! Yet the lessons of surrender didn't always come easily. As I passed each test of surrender, God would give me another.

FALLING BACK

We added worship on Wednesday nights because we believed it would be meaningful to both Christian and non-Christian students. But the majority of our students were not engaged. They didn't understand what it meant to worship. The old "me" would have probably shut down the worship time. But I felt God wanted to challenge us to go deeper and experience him more powerfully. The following week I surprised everyone by extending our worship time and giving students an opportunity to come forward for prayer and confession. While I know this is a common practice for many churches, it wasn't for ours. Because of our church tradition as well as my personal background, emotion and experience were often downplayed, leaving worship far from a deeply moving or meaningful experience.

Somewhere between the idea and the implementation, I fell back on old habits, attempting to coordinate every detail to avoid failure. If we did everything right with music, atmosphere, and timing, the evening would work like magic. On the fateful night, everything was falling into place and the mood was being set. As I finished my lesson, I explained to the students that we would be having an extended time for worship and, when they felt ready, they could come up front for prayer, confession, or spiritual renewal. After singing a few powerful and moving songs, I expected students to start coming forward in droves.

Nobody moved.

I quietly and reverently explained once again the importance of coming forward and how God wanted to meet them there that night. Students remained glued to their seats. I began to sweat. After about thirty minutes of worship, no one had come up for prayer. I gave up and closed with a short prayer. The night was not exactly the deeply moving and powerful experience I had planned.

As you can imagine, I felt like a total idiot for even trying to do something like this. My volunteers offered all kinds of reasonable explanations why no one had come forward, but I was too depressed to listen. I spent the next week thinking and praying about the experience. Then God revealed my mistake. He showed me that I had failed to depend on him to move in the hearts and minds of our students, instead I leaned on my skills and abilities to manipulate the evening. Feeling kicked in the gut once more, I again surrendered my tendency to rely on my power instead of God's.

A few weeks later on a Wednesday night, one of my volunteers encouraged me to give it another try. I wasn't sure if I could take another beating, but I felt God wanted me to trust him, so we went ahead with it. This time there was no fancy programming or special music; I stood before the students and shared how I felt God wanted to do something powerful this night — right here and now. I admitted my awkwardness with such a statement and that I wasn't sure what was going to happen, but that I felt God was leading me to do it. I closed my eyes to pray. When I was done praying, I really didn't want to open my eyes. I imagined everyone sitting around looking at me with blank stares.

When I finally opened my eyes I almost fell over. Standing in front of me were five of the toughest urban guys in the youth group. Not only did they all play varsity football, but they were all bigger than me. With tears in their eyes, they said they needed prayer and wanted to get right with God. For a moment, I felt like the early believers in Acts 12 who prayed fervently for Peter's prison release but couldn't believe it when Peter was physically standing at their door. In the same way, I had a hard time believing these students were standing in front of me asking for prayer. I prayed like I'd never prayed before!

After I finished praying for the guys, I looked around and noticed that the volunteers were each praying with other students. By the end of the night, nearly every student had come forward for prayer and confession. It was one of the most powerful and meaningful experiences we'd ever had. After the night was over, all the leaders marveled at what had happened. There was no doubt in anyone's mind that God had moved in a powerful way. As I drove home that night, I was convicted again of the simple truth that the sooner I get out of the way and allow God to work, the sooner our ministry will see lives transformed and renewed.

God didn't always move in such dramatic and obvious ways. Many times I saw him moving in smaller but just as powerful ways. When an apathetic and obnoxious church kid would suddenly take his faith seriously or when the most hardened and unlikely student would give her life to Christ, I knew it was God. Or when—despite my best efforts to recruit new leaders—God would send volunteers unannounced through our doors that would bless and love our students. In many ways, it was the small and unexpected things God did in our ministry that demonstrated his power best and constantly reminded me of my need to always depend on him.

Because of experiences like this, I began to look at ministry in a whole new way. Instead of trying to predict, plan, and program every little detail, I left room for God to work. I started to anticipate and expect God to show up. Instead of looking at each week as something I had to plan for, I looked forward to seeing how God was going to move. No longer feeling the pressure to make sure everything was a "perfect" success, I was free to take risks and follow his leading. When things didn't work out, I learned to rest in the knowledge that God was in control and that—while I was responsible for doing my part—the results were up to him. I began to experience a new peace and joy as I saw God working *through* my gifts, abilities, and strengths. It wasn't until I was forced to fully depend on God's power that I finally began to understand it.

10 Perfect Leader

Be shepherds of God's flock that is under your care,
serving as overseers — not because you must, but because
you are willing, as God wants you to be; not greedy
for money, but eager to serve; not lording it over those
entrusted to you, but being examples to the flock.

— 1 Peter 5:2-3

WHEN I WAS A CHILD, I USED TO DAYDREAM ABOUT SAVING THE world. Sometimes I saved the world from aliens. Sometimes from scary monsters. And the rest of the time from those generic "bad guys." I had supernatural powers and could fight like Bruce Lee and often used both abilities if the situation was particularly dire. After I'd saved the world, the people would always thank me, and I would be ceremoniously praised as the hero.

As I got older, my daydreams became more focused on wanting to lead others. Whether fighting to be the king of the hill during recess, defending my title in tetherball, or becoming the seventh grade arm wrestling champion, I wanted others to see me as a leader—as someone to look up to and follow. Problem was,

I couldn't find anyone who would follow me. Every time I looked back to see who was with me, nobody was there. I assumed I just wasn't the right kind of leader to warrant followers—something I could change if I became the "perfect" leader. Then people would naturally want to follow me.

This began my quest to find out what it meant to be a perfect leader. When I was growing up, I didn't have any strong role models of what it meant to be a leader, so I was constantly looking for people who could show me. In high school, I looked to professional athletes. In college, I looked to psychologists and counselors—people who held the career I was pursuing. As I felt God calling me into ministry, I began to look to well-known Christian leaders to help me define what "perfect leadership" might look like.

I read *Celebration of Discipline* by Richard Foster first. This convinced me that if I wanted to be a Christian leader, I needed to be a spiritual leader. I needed to be committed to spiritual disciplines such as prayer, solitude, Bible study, and meditation. After reading the chapter on fasting, I was convinced that I needed to fast regularly. The next Monday morning, I got out of bed and decided to fast for the next twenty-four hours. I was feeling pretty good for the first part of the day, but then my stomach started growling. By evening, all I could think about was food. Even watching television that night was painful as I noticed every commercial and TV show that involved food. I managed to make it through the night and eagerly ended my fast the next morning. Somehow, I went on to fast one day a week for several months.

But eventually, I began to lose my commitment to fasting. And my commitment to increased prayer and Bible reading. My ability to "celebrate discipline" waned and I went back to old routines. Not having become the spiritual leader I had hoped to be, I moved on.

Not long after my failure to become the perfect spiritual leader, I came across author and speaker Tony Campolo. Through his writing and teaching, I was challenged to be a Christian leader who sought to care for the poor, hungry, and disadvantaged. At a missions conference in Urbana, Illinois, Tony made the controversial statement, "You can't be a Christian and own a BMW." He went on to explain that a Christian wouldn't spend $60,000 on a car when you could spend far less for a decent car and use the remaining money to feed the hungry and help those in need. I was deeply impacted by this statement, and I began to understand how materialism and consumerism had shaped me. With a newfound passion to impact the world, I sought to be a leader that championed social action, missions, and service. Despite my intentions to change the world, people again weren't lining up to follow my lead. As important as this experience was to my personal development, it didn't help me become the Christian leader I had hoped for.

Next? I came across the writings of Rick Warren. After reading his book *The Purpose-Driven Church*, I was convinced that a Christian leader was someone who understood the importance of growing a church. I started to read and learn everything I could find about planning, strategizing, and programming for church growth. Once

I knew how to grow a ministry, I expected I would become the perfect Christian leader. Once again, I found myself forging ahead without anyone to follow my lead. Sure, some people appreciated my efforts and expertise in church growth, but my preoccupation with growth left others feeling left out or uncared for.

I am nothing if not persistent. The next leader I looked to was Bill Hybels of Willow Creek Church. Starting out a youth pastor, Hybels had a contagious passion for everything he did, from preaching and evangelism to vision casting. What most impressed me about Hybels was his ability to communicate vision in a way that moved people to action. I remember after reading a transcript of a message he gave to his members, I was so moved that I wanted to quit my job and join his church. And then it hit me: A true Christian leader was someone who could motivate and inspire people through vision. I began to learn everything I could about casting vision and calling people to commitment. Unfortunately, my attempts at casting vision were not nearly as successful as Hybels'. Instead of being met with excitement and energy, they were usually met with boredom and apathy. After repeated attempts to inspire people with my vision for our ministry, I gave up.

But I didn't want to give up, so I kept looking to well-known Christian leaders. After a recommendation from a friend, I started reading *Becoming a Person of Influence* by John Maxwell and Jim Dornan. After finishing the book, I was convicted of my need to be a Christian leader who nurtured, connected, and cared for others as a means of developing people. Instead of being a passionate, vision-driven leader, I needed to be a gentle shepherd who looked out for the needs of his flock. Instead of being a leader who understood all the ins and outs of ministry, I needed to be a leader who understood all the ins and outs of people. Instead of being a leader who could speak and communicate well, I needed to be a leader who could listen and empathize well. Well, I may have "needed" to be all these things, but they weren't natural to me and it was difficult to maintain this style of leadership.

To add to my confusion, I started reading the works of Henri Nouwen. Once occupying the highest levels of leadership and influence, Nouwen gave all that up to serve the mentally handicapped. In his book *In the Name of Jesus,* he shared his personal struggle to define himself outside of his accomplishments and abilities as a leader. From this, I began to question my own leadership journey.

Why couldn't I be what I wanted to be?

I had accepted the myth that *I could do anything or be anyone I wanted* with enough effort and hard work. If I wanted to be like Tony Campolo or Richard Foster, I thought I could be. If I wanted to lead like Bill Hybels or John Maxwell, I could do that, too, with enough practice. If I wanted to think and plan like Rick Warren, I could learn how. Because I had been raised in a culture that prided itself on human potential and the ability to overcome any problem or difficulty, I just kept trying harder. It didn't help that almost every book I read or seminar I went to communicated the same myth.

I thought I could transform any weakness into a strength. For years I had tried this with my (sadly lacking) organizational skills. I read books on time management, bought tons of Day-Timers, and implemented sophisticated organizational systems. I always ended up back where I started—with piles of paper on my desk and a bulletin board that had more in common with "pin the tail on the donkey" than any kind of filing system. The same was true with my weakness of not being able to read people's emotions and nonverbals. I've been married for over twelve years and my wife still has to "spell it out" for me when I don't get it. As much as I have tried to transform this weakness into a strength, I haven't magically become more sensitive and attuned to their emotions. I still miss obvious clues.

I was so focused on trying to be someone else that I was blind to who I really was as a leader. I stopped looking at my weaknesses and asked the question, "What are my strengths as a leader?" I couldn't answer the question right away, but simply asking it changed the way I looked at what it means to be a leader.

UNDERSTANDING MY STRENGTHS

The StrengthsFinder, developed by the Gallup Organization, helped provide clarity for me regarding my unique strengths. Based on interviews with over two million people who demonstrated excellence in their chosen fields, Gallup discovered thirty-four common "themes" of talents among individuals. They defined a talent as a "recurring pattern of thought, feeling, or behavior that can be productively applied." Unlike skills and knowledge that are learned, talents can't be learned and are unique to each person. When a talent is combined with the right knowledge and skills, it becomes a strength that allows a person to experience "consistent near perfect performance in an activity."

I learned that one of my talents was "ideation"—a fascination with ideas and concepts. It explained why it was natural for me to come to a meeting or brainstorming session with an overabundance of ideas. It also clarified why I was good at finding patterns and connections among seemingly dissimilar or contradictory facts. This is why I enjoyed learning conflicting views on a given subject and then synthesizing them into a coherent model. It explained why I felt a need for everything to "fit together" with every decision and action rooted in the same theory or concept.

Coupled with my talent of "input," which was a craving to learn more through collecting information, this clarified why I love to read so much. It made sense why the more I read and learned about youth ministry, the more excited and energized I became. It also made sense why when I got too busy to read, I would start to lose energy. And I finally understood why I was one of the few youth workers who loved bringing ministry books on vacation.

Another talent revealed by the StrengthsFinder was "restorative," described as a love of solving problems. So that's why I had always sought churches with youth ministries that were broken down and in deep need of repair! I saw these situations as opportunities to turn things around. Instead of being drained by problems, I was energized by opportunities to find a solution and restore something to its original glory.

The most revealing insight from my StrengthsFinder was my talent of "command." People with this talent like to take control of situations and make decisions. They aren't afraid to share their opinions and present the facts even if others are avoiding it. They want things to be clear between them and others and like to push people to take risks. Rather than fearing confrontation, they often see it as a first step toward resolution. When I read the description for command, my first thought was, "This is my life!" My second thought was, "Are you sure this is a talent?"

In church environments where politics rule the day, my "talent" for command had caused me to step on many land mines. I learned the hard way that in these environments, it was far too easy for me to commit political suicide just by opening my mouth. When someone needed me to listen or be supportive, my tendency was to be *too* honest and tell them more than they needed to hear. My comfort with conflict and confrontation caused some people to feel threatened and intimidated. Of all my talents, I struggled the most to accept this one.

Command had been a strength in the right situations. After arriving at one church where the youth ministry was having serious discipline problems, I took control of the situation quickly. Students were regularly coming and leaving youth group as they pleased. Students "ditching" youth group became a serious problem. After being dropped off in front of the church by their parents, some students would avoid the church altogether and go directly to the mall across the street instead. This had been going on for quite a while, but nobody had done anything about it.

I started keeping track of all the students and making sure we found any who may have gotten "lost" during the night. I kept a close watch at the front of the church when kids were dropped off. If students took off to the mall, I contacted their parents immediately and notified them. Even though I knew that many of these students would never come back to youth group again, I figured they weren't interested in coming to youth group in the first place.

I let students know clearly what was and wasn't appropriate behavior. I didn't mind being the disciplinarian. While I didn't enjoy asking disrespectful students to leave, I knew it was the right thing to do. Fortunately, many of these students returned with a different attitude after a few weeks. Because of my strength in command, I was able to take control, make the tough decisions, and confront inappropriate behaviors when necessary. Things did settle down and youth group became a safe and positive place. Students even started liking me again.

GROWING IN MY STRENGTHS

Understanding my talents explained a lot of things for me. I realized part of my problem in leadership was thinking what came naturally to me would come naturally to others. A lightbulb went on in my head when I recognized how I had been unwittingly projecting onto others my natural talents.

Things changed when I saw people through *their* talents instead of mine. I began to see my wife through her talent of "harmony" and stopped becoming frustrated when I saw her willingly avoid conflict for the sake of progress and efficiency. For years I had thought she was letting people take advantage of her, but now I realized that she had a gift of "going with the flow" or finding the "common ground." And when I recognized my friend's talent of empathy, I understood why he could perceive things about people's emotions I couldn't. I stopped accusing him of being too sensitive and discovered instead his unique talent for discerning what people were feeling. Something which will never become natural for me.

Here's another significant lesson in all of this: You can't use your talents as excuses for poor leadership. My talent in fixing problems and moving quickly often led me to emphasize results at the expense of relationships. Instead of taking the time to listen, be patient, and bring people along in the journey, I tended to move decisively, wounding people in the process. Putting the blame on others, I rationalized that they were resistant to change and didn't want to move the ministry forward. But now I realize that I need to be more patient and willing to slow down so I can listen to others and consider their thoughts and feelings.

While it's natural for me to take charge of a situation and confront issues head-on, I've had to recognize that this isn't always the best course of action. Like a bull in a china shop, I can break more things than I fix. When the situation requires diplomacy and tact, I need to rely on others for wisdom and guidance. If I'm working with people who are sensitive, I need to adjust my approach so I don't intimidate or overwhelm them. And if I'm leading people who are more relational than task-oriented, I need to prioritize time for relationship building and community. Before I figured this out, I had to learn the painful lesson that just because I'm comfortable with being direct and taking charge doesn't mean I should express this talent with every person or in every situation.

LIVING MY STRENGTHS

One of my professors often said, "Stand in your strengths and lean into your weaknesses." Standing in our strengths gives us confidence and fulfillment whereas standing in our weaknesses makes us feel anxious and frustrated.

Standing in my strengths meant understanding that my greatest area of growth was not in my weaknesses, but in my strengths. I needed to focus my energy on developing my talents to their fullest potential. For example, instead of feeling guilty for wanting to constantly read and learn about ministry, I needed to build up this talent by dedicating more time to it so I could pass on to others what I was learning.

When I do have to lead from my weaknesses, I should only "lean into" them temporarily. Because leaning involves being off balance, I can't stay there long before I become unstable. My professor's point was that while I can't ignore my weaknesses, I shouldn't spend all day standing there either. I need the respective strengths of others to help counterbalance my weaknesses. In concert, when we all lead together with our strengths, then our weaknesses become irrelevant.

I could not save the world on my own. Even with supernatural powers and Bruce Lee-like skills, I couldn't become the perfect leader. As it turns out, there is no such thing. There are lots of good leaders. I've learned from all of them. Yet by trying to be Tony Campolo, Bill Hybels, Rick Warren, and John Maxwell, I wasn't being the leader God wanted.

I wasn't being David Chow.

And that was exactly who God wanted me to be.

11 Perfect Ending

*Consider it pure joy, my brothers, whenever you face
trials of many kinds, because you know that the testing
of your faith develops perseverance.
Perseverance must finish its work so that you may be
mature and complete, not lacking anything.*

— James 1:2-4

"YOU'RE FIRED!"

With those two words, Donald Trump would send away one of the potential winners of the popular reality TV show *Apprentice*, usually for messing up on a project or not being a strong enough leader. Or for making too many enemies. In youth ministry, I always thought people were fired because they'd done something illegal, committed an immoral act, or were incompetent. If I avoided these errors, it would never happen to me.

That is . . . until it happened to me.

I was completely unprepared when the church asked me to resign. It felt like the sudden death of a close friend. Up until this point, I had always left a church on good terms. It seemed like things were going great at the church, but then, everything changed.

I was in denial. For the first time in my ministry career, I felt frozen and unable to move. Like a deer caught in headlights, I didn't know whether to run or stand still.

I opted for "damage control." My reputation was at stake. A negative departure from such a notable church would surely affect how others saw me. I decided to minimize the damage by putting a positive spin on the situation. I sent an e-mail to all my friends and associates telling them that I had a new e-mail address once the church e-mail address was no longer valid. Yet instead of being honest about the situation and giving background on why I had a new e-mail address, I didn't say anything about what happened at the church.

Because the church had not technically fired me, but had given me the option to resign, I led some people to believe I had simply chosen to move on. While I felt this was appropriate for the students because I didn't want them to resent the church for my departure, I should have been more upfront with others.

I tried avoiding the issue. Except with my closest friends, I had a hard time talking openly about what had happened. I started to avoid people I would normally keep in touch with, and when I did run into them, I did everything I could to dodge the subject of my departure. I wish I would have had the maturity to worry less about what others thought and instead been real and transparent with them.

After the initial shock, I began to feel a loss of identity. I had now lost my point of reference. No longer serving at a church,

I wasn't sure how to define myself. When people would ask me what I did for a living, I struggled. "Am I still a pastor even if I don't have a church?" "Does this experience mean I'm no longer called to youth ministry?" "If I don't go back to the church, what else will I do?" As I struggled with a loss of identity, I yearned to be back in ministry at a church.

I was tempted to jump right back into ministry for all the wrong reasons. I now understand why people often short-circuit the grieving process after losing someone or something important to them — instead of accepting the loss, it's easier to swiftly replace the loss with something else or deny the pain.

It was difficult to sort through my emotions. At times I blamed myself and took all the responsibility for how things had turned out. "If I had done everything right, this wouldn't have happened." I began to question all that I'd done at the church. I started to doubt my adequacy as a youth worker. I began to question all the positive years in ministry and wondered if I had just deceived myself. I even questioned my very calling into youth ministry.

At other times, I was angry at the church. "Was it even appropriate for the church to fire me over such issues?" "Why couldn't the church have tried to find a solution before taking such steps?" "Why didn't I have any warning that this was going to happen?" The more I thought about these questions, the angrier I became. I substituted my feelings of doubt and insecurity with anger and resentment toward the church. *I* was the victim.

If you've ever been asked to leave a job of any kind, you know an additional pain — the pain of rumor and innuendo that follows in the wake of your departure. I had never experienced the backlash that happens when a person is asked to leave. I knew there were many people who appreciated me and my ministry, but the words that sounded loudest came from people who had negative feelings toward me and were glad to see me go.

My emotions vacillated between anger and depression. Sometimes I would flip back and forth how I felt within the same day. Having always been a very rational person, it was strange to feel such powerful and extreme emotions having their way with me. There was no way to "think" my way through this; I had to accept my daily emotional roller coaster as I tried to sort out my feelings.

I came to a decision point: Did I want to allow this experience to make me a "bitter" person or make me a "better" person? If I spent all my energy focusing on what others had done wrong, I knew I would end up becoming bitter and angry. I would spend the rest of my life blaming others for my problems. Even though I had never seen myself as a bitter person, I could easily see myself going down this path.

If I wanted to be a better person, I would need to see this experience as a time for growth and learning. Like in the book of James, I needed to let this "trial" make me more mature and complete in Christ. I had to trust that God would use this experience for his glory. This is easier said than done. The real test wouldn't be whether I had a "proper theology" on trials and suffering, but whether I was willing to let go of the hurt and anger and trust God to redeem it.

After much wrestling, I made the right choice. It wasn't an easy decision. It didn't help that my wife was having a harder time with the situation than I was. Because she was more removed from the situation, her anger was stronger—she didn't understand why the church had acted the way it did. My wife had been a faithful supporter and servant of the church. As we worked through this together, we concluded that God wanted to use this experience in a positive way in our lives. But because being angry was easier than being humble, we had to rely on God's grace and strength to keep us teachable and moldable.

I COULDN'T DO IT ALONE

I needed the help of mentors who could help me navigate this difficult experience. I hadn't really taken seriously the need for mentors in my life. In the past, I was arrogant enough to think I could figure things out on my own and what I couldn't figure out, I could learn from books and seminars. But this time there was no way I could make it through this ordeal on my own.

The first mentor I sought out was a pastor I had worked with. Terry and I had formed a close friendship, and because he understood the situation, I felt safe around him. I knew he wouldn't hold back from speaking the truth into my life. I asked him if he would be willing to meet with me every other week. Thankfully, he agreed and God started me on an important journey in my life.

Being older and wiser, Terry helped me see things about myself I had overlooked. He challenged me to think about how different people responded to me. He wanted me to realize that not everyone works well with someone like me. My intense drive and emphasis on results was too much for some people. Instead of being a source of inspiration and challenge, it became for them a source of frustration and misunderstanding. My style of leadership left highly relational people believing that I only cared about what they produced or how hard they worked. Terry wanted me to see that because of the way I'm wired, I shouldn't expect everyone else to work like I did. And because I can't *change* the way I'm wired, I need to be more discerning about the people I choose to surround myself with.

Terry encouraged me to think about the emotional side of leadership. It was during this time that I read *Primal Leadership* by Daniel Goleman. Popularizing the term "Emotional Intelligence" or EI, Goleman argued that many leaders have emphasized the IQ or the "cognitive" side of leadership at the expense of the "emotional" side of leadership. Leaders with low emotional intelligence were often out of touch with themselves and the people they led. I felt like a Mack truck had hit me, as it brought into focus many things I had failed to see.

For example, I had failed to develop such things as self-awareness and self-management. Because I lacked self-awareness, I couldn't see how my emotions made others feel when they were around me. If I had had insight into this, I might not have missed the warning signs. Compounded by a lack of self-management, I had failed to manage the stress in my life and my stress started leaking into my interactions with people. Rather than bringing out the best in me, it brought out the worst.

It wasn't until I left the church that I realized just how negative and overwhelming stress had been on me. As my stress began to dissipate, I went through what felt like a personality change as I began to relate to people in a more relaxed and calm manner. My wife even commented how happy she was to have "gotten her husband back." Having had to learn the hard way what can happen when I don't manage my stress, I've become a lot more aware of my limitations and how easily stress can spill over into my relationships with others.

LEADERSHIP COACHING

Understanding emotional intelligence was a big step for me. But not the only step I would need to find my way through. So I sought the help of another mentor, Dan Webster. Twenty years earlier, Dan had been the youth pastor at the church I had just left. From there, he'd led an incredible youth ministry at Willow Creek Church for over ten years. I looked up to Dan and was a fan of his teaching. After leaving Willow Creek, he focused on coaching and training leaders through his ministry organization, Authentic Leadership, Inc.

I poured out my heart for over an hour the first time we talked since my departure. He affirmed me for trying to learn as much as I could from this experience and helped me realize that because I'm a cause-driven leader, I thrive best in churches that are continually growing, changing, and focusing on their mission. Those simple words brought a lot of clarity to my situation.

He agreed to coach me through this experience, and shortly after that I flew out to Michigan to spend two days with him. He helped me understand how I had compartmentalized leadership. I had seen leadership as something you "do" instead of something you "are"—I had separated the act of leadership from the personhood of leadership. Dan encouraged me to move toward becoming someone who led from the inside out. This could only happen by my allowing God to shape and mold me into the leader he created me to be.

Seeing leadership as being an inside-out process has helped me understand that authentic leaders aren't simply focused on developing the right skills or abilities, but on developing the right heart and character. Dan challenged me to allow God to use this time to deepen my character and discover God's vision for my life.

I didn't jump right back into ministry. I wanted to, but Dan challenged me to think seriously about each opportunity. I asked him many times, "Are you sure I shouldn't take this job?" His typical response was, "Dave, there will always be leadership opportunities. Now is not the time to be pursuing them." I knew he was right—that God wasn't finished working on me, but I felt a bit like a "sidelined" athlete.

The book *Understanding Leadership* by Tom Marshall taught me something significant about leadership. Marshall looked at the life of Jesus and specifically Philippians 2:5-7, which teaches us,

> *Your attitude should be the same as that of Christ Jesus:*
> *Who, being in very nature God, did not consider equality*

> with God something to be grasped, but made himself
> nothing, _taking the very nature of a servant_, being made in
> human likeness. (emphasis added)

Marshall made the case that Christian leaders need to be _servants by nature_ and not by responsibility. I had always seen myself as a _leader by nature_ and a servant by responsibility. I had always seen serving others as part of my role as a leader but never as part of my nature. This insight helped me understand why some Christian leaders stop serving the higher they climb in leadership.

I needed to be a servant by nature. If I'm truly a servant by nature, then leading others will always be an act of service and not of power, influence, or authority. This was an important truth for me to grasp and I discovered it during a season — the first time since I had gone into ministry — when I _wasn't_ in a leadership position. God wanted to teach me what it meant to be a servant without being a leader.

At the church I started attending, I began volunteering in non-leadership capacities. It was a new experience for me to support those in leadership. I regained my joy for ministry and appreciation for the incredible privilege of serving God and others.

An interesting thing started happening. As I learned to serve without leading, God began to bring leadership opportunities my way — an opportunity to coach a leader, to speak on leadership issues, or to help equip a church. Little by little, God showed me he still wanted to use me for his purposes. Every time God would open a door for me, I could hear Dan saying, "I told you so. Be patient—you're not out of the game. God still wants to use you."

It's been a long road, but I now understand why God didn't ask me to be a psychologist or a paramedic. He has taught me the importance of being an emotionally intelligent leader. He has shown me the environments where my talents, personality, and skills can make the greatest difference. He has coached me on how to be an authentic leader—someone who sees leading others as an expression of my "being" and not "doing." And most importantly, he has shown me how to be a servant first . . . and leader second.

There is no perfect program. No perfect leader. There are no perfect kids or parents. And there is no perfect ending. But I am learning, through all of this, that God is perfecting me to be the person he created me to be.

And that sounds just perfect to me.

Notes

1. Andy Stanley, *The Next Generation Leader* (Sisters, Ore.: Multnomah, 2003), 42.
2. Kenda Creasy Dean and Ron Foster, *The Godbearing Life* (Nashville, Tenn.: Upper Room Books, 1998), 42.
3. Lance Armstrong with Sally Jenkins, *It's Not About the Bike* (New York: Berkley, 2001), 265.
4. Richard Farson and Ralph Keyes, *Whoever Makes the Most Mistakes Wins* (New York: Free Press, 2002), 3, 6-7.

Author

DAVID CHOW is a veteran youth worker with fifteen years of experience "in the trenches." He is the author of *No More Lone Rangers* and a frequent speaker on leadership and youth ministry issues. He is the founder of Leading Together (www.leadingtogether.com), an organization that coaches leaders and equips churches. He has a master's in organizational leadership from Biola University and lives in Southern California with his wife and two children.

GET YOUR SMALL GROUPS TALKING.

THINK (((OutLoud!

THINK™ OutLoud! is a small-group learning experience that doesn't involve charades, ropes courses, or the throwing of marshmallows.

THINK OutLoud: Renovation of the Heart

Based on the foundational principles from Dallas Willard's book *Renovation of the Heart*, this resource will encourage your students to experience a complete renovation of the heart, mind, body, social life, and soul.
Dallas Willard and Randy Frazee   1-57683-924-9

THINK OutLoud: Posers, Fakers & Wannabes

Based on the fundamental principles from Brennan Manning's books *Abba's Child* and *Posers, Fakers, and Wannabes*, this book will help students see how God's grace sets them free—free to be who they really are.
Brennan Manning and Jim Hancock   1-57683-799-8

Visit your local Christian bookstore,
call NavPress at 1-800-366-7788, or log on to www.navpress.com
to purchase.

To locate a Christian bookstore near you,
call 1-800-991-7747.

NAVPRESS ®
BRINGING TRUTH TO LIFE
www.navpress.com

259.23
C5527P

LINCOLN CHRISTIAN COLLEGE AND SEMINARY

1/2277

3 4711 00176 7047